AA

LEISURE GUIDE

Peak District

Author: Mike Gerrard
Verifier: Neil Coates
Managing Editor: David Popey
Project Management: Bookwork Creative Associates Ltd
Designers: Liz Baldin of Bookwork and Andrew Milne
Picture Library Manager: Ian Little
Picture Research: Vivien Little and Michelle Aylott
Cartography provided by the Mapping Services Department of AA Publishing
Copy-editors: Marilynne Lanng of Bookwork and Pamela Stagg
Internal Repro and Image Manipulation: Jacqueline Street
Production: Rachel Davis

Produced by AA Publishing

Reprinted 2008
Updated and revised 2010

Published by AA Publishing (a trading name of AA Media Limited, whose registered office is Fanum House, Basing View, Basingstoke, Hampshire RG21 4EA; registered number 06112600).

ISBN 978-0-7495-6692-0
ISBN 978-0-7495-6705-7 (SS)

A CIP catalogue record for this book is available from the British Library.

Printed and bound in China by C&C

A04393

CONTENTS

Welcome to the...
Peak District

INTRODUCTION

It has been called The Hollow Country. It is an extraordinary landscape riven by gorges and riddled by caverns where lowland England erupts into upland splendour, haltered by endless miles and countless acres of bronze and purple-burnished moors, cliffs and scarps arcing to the horizon to meet with England's backbone, the lofty Pennines.

The heart of England's first National Park is the White Peak, reflecting the pale-grey hues of the limestone bedrock. Beyond the gaping maw of Dovedale are undulating plateaux dotted by prehistoric monuments and threaded by field walls; here ash woods cascade into spectacular valleys where seasonal rivers flow with crystal-clear water in winter and green veins of butterbur during summer. Beneath villages of silvery cottages set in abundant wildflower meadows, miners toiled for centuries, turning the landscape inside-out, discovering cave systems and unwittingly creating fascinating heritage locations that melt seamlessly into the backcloth.

Around the north, east and west of this timeless core sweep stunning escarpments and ridges of millstone grit, a rugged geological formation giving us the name of the Dark Peak. Vast moors dappled by reservoirs end in precipitous edges, over which waterfalls tumble into wooded vales that once echoed to the thrumming of industry. Here were the world's first great textile mills, England's own silk industry and countless other enterprises that make the Peak a peerless area for industrial archaeology. Tucked below the scalloped edges of these moors are charming small towns and villages of three-storey weaver's cottages and soot-darkened church towers, where narrowboat trips offer ease of exploration whilst paths snake up to boundless moors haunted by white hares and the chuckling of grouse.

Traversing this former tribal domain – Peak comes from the Dark Ages clan, the pecsaetan – are Britain's first and latest National Trails, the Pennine Way and Pennine Bridleway. Myriad other trails and walks combine with trekking country, cycling routes, many based on former packhorse trails and railways drawing together past and present.

Scratch the surface and the land that charmed and terrified authors and commentators from Daniel Defoe to George Eliot, Sir Arthur Conan Doyle to D H Lawrence is still there for the finding. The Hollow Country and its darker twin can enlighten and excite, educate and exhilarate.

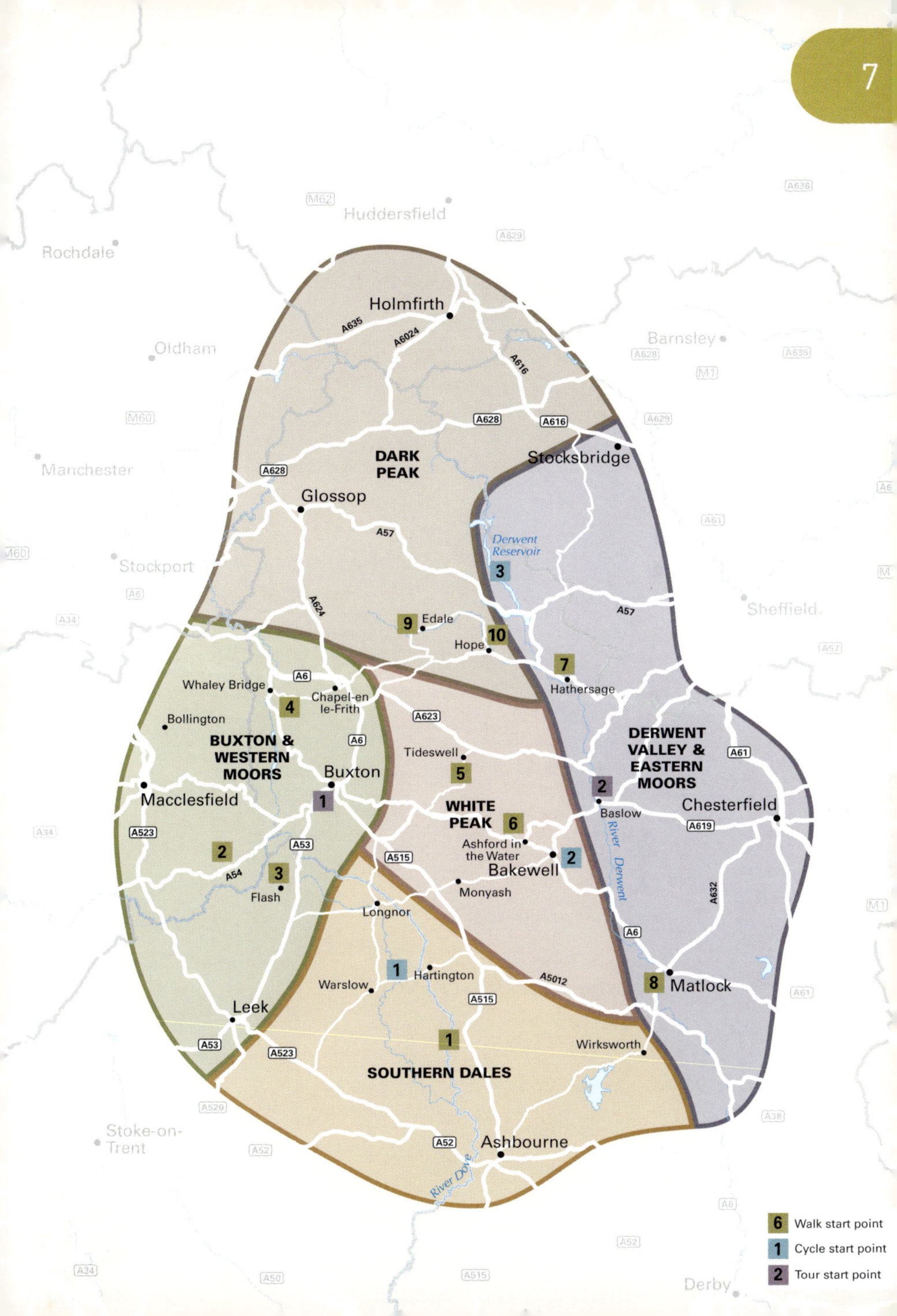

Huddersfield
Rochdale
Holmfirth
Oldham
Barnsley
Manchester
Stocksbridge
DARK PEAK
Glossop
Stockport
Derwent Reservoir
Sheffield
Edale
Hope
Hathersage
Whaley Bridge
Chapel-en le-Frith
Bollington
BUXTON & WESTERN MOORS
Buxton
Macclesfield
Tideswell
WHITE PEAK
DERWENT VALLEY & EASTERN MOORS
Baslow
Chesterfield
River Derwent
Ashford in the Water
Bakewell
Monyash
Flash
Longnor
Hartington
Warslow
Matlock
Leek
Wirksworth
SOUTHERN DALES
Stoke-on-Trent
Ashbourne
River Dove
Derby
6 Walk start point
1 Cycle start point
2 Tour start point

1

2

Essential Sights

The Peak District, covering 555sq miles (1,438sq km), was designated as England's first National Park in 1951, reflecting its importance as a landscape of rare drama and beauty. Lead mining has left a legacy of discarded millstones and farming has shaped the open moors and created drystone-wall pastures. No other region of England has such diversity, busy with visitors and walkers yet full of wide open spaces where walkers, although close to large towns and cities, can feel as though they are at one with the wilderness.

3

1 **Leek**
Enjoy far-reaching views, which take in green fields divided by drystone walls while gentle slopes lead down to the valley bottom in the countryside near the Roaches.

2 **Kinder Scout**
A hiker scrambles over gritstone slabs high above Kinder Reservoir at the western fringe of the Dark Peak. Tracks from nearby Hayfield climb steeply to the magnificent, moody plateau of Kinder Scout, the highest point in the National Park.

3 **Stepping Stones across the River Dove**
Here, at the southern end of Dovedale, just east of the village of Ilam, are the stepping stones that cross the River Dove. This beauty spot is hugely popular with families who like to picnic near the banks of the river.

4 Edale
A popular centre with walkers and hikers, Edale sits quietly in a paradise of pasture, riverside meadow and hedgerow, surrounded by high moors. It is also the start of the Pennine Way, Britain's most famous long-distance footpath.

5 Blue John Cavern & Mine
This remarkable example of a water-worn cave contains veins of eight of the 14 known varieties of the beautiful Blue John stone. You can explore the mine on a guided tour.

6 Kinder Plateau
A blanket of wet peat covers the exposed Kinder plateau – a wild and lonely part of the moor. National Park rangers lead guided walks throughout the year to many areas of the Park.

7 Dovedale
This is one of the most beautiful and popular of all the limestone dales, with paths that range over windswept grassland hills to the deep shadows of the valley.

8 Ashbourne
Lively markets are a feature of many of the towns in the Peak District. In Ashbourne traders set up their stalls in Market Place on Thursday and Saturday.

PUBLIC
FOOTPATH ONLY
MILLDALE
& DOVEDALE

7

SMITHS TAVERN
ASHBOURNE
TRAIL
THE COB STOP

8

LADYBOWER RESERVOIR

DAY ONE

For many people a weekend break or a long weekend is a popular way to spend their leisure time. These four pages offer a loosely planned itinerary designed to ensure that you make the most of your time and see and enjoy the very best the area has to offer.

Friday Night

If you can afford it, stay at Fischer's Baslow Hall hotel, just north of Baslow village on the A623, perched above the River Derwent. The food is superb: herbs freshly picked from the kitchen garden and succulent local venison, pork, beef and pigeon. In the evening you can go for a short drive and stroll on to Curbar Edge, for a view of the setting sun over the White Peak.

Saturday Morning

On the A619 is the impressive entrance to Chatsworth Park. Spend the morning walking around the magnificent house and grounds, or explore East Moor and Beeley Moor. Here, you will fine excellent heather moorland, with Bronze Age settlements and barrows.

Return to Baslow and rejoin the A623, driving northwest up Middleton Dale, past Lovers' Leap and Baslow's tiny octagonal toll house.

Saturday Lunch

Stop at the Three Stags Head pub at Wardlow Mires. This stone-floored pub serves well-kept beers from excellent independent Sheffield breweries. You'll find good food too, served on plates and dishes from the adjacent pottery.

Saturday Afternoon

Head for Tideswell, either by driving further along the A623 and turning off left, or by a side-road through the pretty village of Litton. Walk round the fine parish church at Tideswell ('Cathedral of the Peak') then take the car down to the Tideswell Dale car park and walk along Miller's Dale as far as Water-cum-Jolly Dale, with ash trees, limestone crags and the tinkling waters of the Wye.

Drive southwest on the B6049 and A5270 to meet the A515 and then go southeast to Parsley Hay. Turn left on minor roads for Youlgreave for a look at the great stone circle of Arbor Low – a ditch, bank and circle of 47 stones, now lying flat – and the nearby barrow of Gib Hill; both date from the Bronze Age. Return to the A515 and turn left; then right onto the B5054 to Hartington.

Saturday Night

Stay at Biggin Hall, located just 1 mile (1.6km) to the southeast of Hartington; it comprises a cluster of 17th-century buildings with mullioned windows and oak beams. If possible, try to book the Master Suite, complete with four-poster bed. In the morning, enjoy a traditional farmhouse breakfast using good locally produced ingredients.

DAY TWO

You are in the heart of the White Peak, close to the southern dales. Your second day explores this beautiful area before heading north for a tour of the Dark Peak, with alternative options depending on your personal preferences and the weather.

Sunday Morning

Go for an early walk down Biggin Dale, or linger over breakfast and then look round Hartington; feed the ducks on the pond and buy some local cheese to take home. Then follow in the footsteps of the 'Compleat Anglers', Izaak Walton and Charles Cotton, down Beresford Dale on the quiet upper reaches of the River Dove. You can walk as far as you wish, into Wolfscote Dale and to Mill Dale, but for this you will need a packed lunch.

Further south still is famous Dovedale. If you wish you can drive to Ilam and take the easy short walk by the Stepping Stones to Mill Dale. But remember, this route is likely to be popular on a fine Sunday morning.

Sunday Lunch

From Hartington or Ilam head for Warslow (on the B5053), where you can call in for lunch at the Greyhound Inn, a traditional coaching inn popular for its home-cooked dishes. Warslow is close to the Manifold Valley; a short detour down minor roads into Ecton will give you a flavour of the scenery, and there is a visitor centre at the nearby old station at Hulme End.

Sunday Afternoon

Leaving Warslow, drive north on the A5053 to and through Longnor to reach the A515; here turn left to Buxton.

There are now several options. If the weather is really unkind you can spend the afternoon here, breezing around the Pavilion Gardens or visiting Poole's Cavern. Return to Baslow via the A6 south, Bakewell and then the A619.

Alternatively, head north on the A6 through Dove Holes, turn right onto the A623 and then fork left at The Wanted Inn to reach Castleton via the dramatic Winnats Pass road. In Castleton, there are caves and Blue John mines, the oldest castle in the Peak and good pubs and cafés.

Or, if you are feeling adventurous and there is no risk of blizzards stay on the A6 north to Chapel-en-le-Frith then north on the A624 to Glossop.Turn east on the A57, crossing the Snake Pass and dropping down the Woodlands Valley to the Derwent Dams. Whichever way you go, finish at Padley Gorge (Grindleford) close to where you started, in the shade of sessile oaks and with pied flycatchers singing among the branches.

DOVEDALE

WINNATS PASS, CASTLETON

Route facts

MINIMUM TIME The time stated for completing each route is the estimated minimum time that a reasonably fit family group of walkers or cyclists would take to complete the circuit. This does not allow for rest or refreshment stops.

OS MAP Each route is shown on a map. However, some detail is lost because of the restrictions imposed by scale, so for this reason, we recommend that you use the maps in conjunction with a more detailed Ordnance Survey map. The relevant map for each walk or cycle ride is listed.

START This indicates the start location and parking area. This is a six-figure grid reference prefixed by two letters showing which 62.5-mile (100km) square of the National Grid it refers to. You'll find more information on grid references on most Ordnance Survey maps.

CYCLE HIRE We list, within reason, the nearest cycle hire shop/centre.

❶ Here we highlight any potential difficulties or dangers along the cycle ride or walk. If a particular route is suitable for older, fitter children we say so here. Also, we give guidelines of a route's suitability for younger children, for example the symbol 8+ indicates that the route can probably be attempted by children aged 8 years and above.

Walks & Cycle Rides

Each walk and cycle ride has a panel giving information for the walker and cyclist, including the distance, terrain, nature of the paths, and where to park your car.

WALKING

All of the walks are suitable for families, but less experienced family groups, especially those with younger children, should try the shorter walks. Route finding is usually straightforward, but the maps are for guidance only and we recommend that you always take the relevant Ordnance Survey map with you.

Risks

Although each walk has been researched with a view to minimising any risks, no walk in the countryside can be considered to be completely free from risk. Walking in the outdoors will always require a degree of common sense and judgement to ensure that it is as safe as possible, especially for young children.

- Be particularly careful on cliff paths and in upland terrain, where the consequences of a slip can be serious.
- Remember to check tidal conditions before walking on the seashore.
- Some sections of route are by, or cross, busy roads. Remember traffic is a danger even on minor country lanes.
- Be careful around farmyard machinery and livestock.
- Be prepared for the consequences of changes in the weather and check the forecast before you set out.
- Ensure the whole family is properly equipped, wearing suitable clothing and a good pair of boots or sturdy walking shoes. Take waterproof clothing with you and a torch if you are walking in the winter months.
- Remember the weather can change quickly at any time of the year, and in moorland and heathland areas, mist and fog can make route-finding much harder. In summer, take account of the heat and sun by wearing a hat, sunscreen and carrying enough water.
- On walks away from centres of population you should carry a mobile phone, whistle and, if possible, a survival bag. If you do have an accident requiring emergency services, make a note of your position as accurately as possible and dial 999 (112 on a mobile).

CYCLING

In devising the cycle rides in this guide, every effort has been made to use designated cycle paths, or to link them with quiet country lanes and waymarked byways and bridleways. In a few cases, some fairly busy B-roads have been used to join up with quieter routes.

Rules of the road

- Ride in single file on narrow and busy roads.
- Be alert, look and listen for traffic, especially on narrow lanes and blind bends and be extra careful when descending steep hills, as loose gravel or a poor road surface can lead to an accident.
- In wet weather make sure that you keep an appropriate distance between you and other riders.
- Make sure you indicate your intentions clearly.
- Brush up on *The Highway Code* before venturing out onto the road.

Off-road safety code of conduct

- Only ride where you know it is legal to do so. Cyclists are not allowed to cycle on public footpaths (yellow waymarks). The only 'rights of way' open to cyclists are bridleways (blue markers) and unsurfaced tracks, known as byways, which are open to all traffic and waymarked in red.
- Canal tow paths: you need a permit to cycle on some stretches of tow path (www.waterscape.com). Remember that access paths can be steep and slippery so always push your bike under low bridges and by locks.
- Always yield to walkers and horses, giving adequate warning of your approach.
- Don't expect to cycle at high speeds.
- Keep to the main trail to avoid any unnecessary erosion to the area beside the trail and to prevent skidding, especially in wet weather conditions.
- Remember to follow the Country Code.

Preparing your bicycle

Check the wheels, tyres, brakes and cables. Lubricate hubs, pedals, gear mechanisms and cables. Make sure you have a pump, a bell, a rear rack to carry panniers and a set of lights.

Equipment

- A cycling helmet provides essential protection.
- Make sure you are visible to other road users, by wearing light-coloured or luminous clothing in daylight and sashes or reflective strips in failing light and darkness.
- Take extra clothes with you, depending on the season, and a wind/waterproof jacket.
- Carry a basic tool kit, a pump, a strong lock and a first aid kit.
- Always carry enough water for your outing.

Walk Map Legend

– – ➔ – –	Route		Built-up Area
1	Route Waypoint		Woodland Area
— — — —	Adjoining Path		Toilet
	Viewpoint	P [P]	Car Park
•	Place of interest		Picnic Area
	Steep Section	START	Cycle Start Point
	Picnic Area		

DOVEDALE

Southern Dales

INTRODUCTION

Middle England meets the North as you walk or drive uphill from Ashbourne Market Place. The arc of countryside from Leek through Ashbourne to Belper pays its dues to the Trent; it rolls and dips southwards to the river plain and its tributary, the Dove, meanders gracefully through green fields and hedgerows. But on the far side of Ashbourne everything changes as the land rises and the Dove spreads out a thousand fingers into every crevice of the hills. Brooks and rivulets reach into the limestone at the Peak's core. Villages lie on the thousand-foot contour on the plateau because the valleys are so narrow; ancient ash woods clothe the slopes, dairy cattle graze the pastures and drystone walls cobweb the meadows.

TISSINGTON

MANIFOLD VALLEY

Unmissable attractions

Ashbourne, a market town, celebrated for its gingerbread, is at the gateway to Dovedale, the most famous and popular of all the dales. This 7-mile (11.3km) stretch, from the Stepping Stones to Hartington is best avoided at peak holiday times but the quieter upper reaches can be explored from the little hilltop village of Longnor, which sits atop a ridge between the Dove and Manifold. There are many good walks from this charming village, including the reef limestone hills of Chrome and High Wheeldon to the east. Just to the south is the twisting gorge of the Manifold Valley, which has one of several cycle rides that follow the tracks of disused railways.

1

2

1 Ashbourne
St Oswald's Church in Ashbourne with its tall spire (212 feet/65m), is one of Derbyshire's grandest.

2 Dovedale
A path follows the River Dove as it winds its way below the limestone peaks.

3 Manifold Valley
Spectacular Thor's Cave dominates the centre of the Manifold Valley.

4 Carsington Water
Popular with sailors of all ages and abilities, Carsington Water also has a network of walking and cycling trails.

ASHBOURNE MAP REF SK1746

The old market town of Ashbourne is located in a cleft in the rolling farmland of southwest Derbyshire, a landscape of fields and hedges rather than moors and walls. Along this green cleft runs the Henmore Brook on its way to meet the River Dove.

The drive into and through Ashbourne is not straightforward; there is a one-way system and the roads are often congested, but there are points on the sweeping drive down into the town where the shape of the settlement can be appreciated. The most immediate impression is that the parish church, with its distinctive needle-sharp spire, is some way from the town centre. This means that when you have parked your car, there is a walk of several hundred yards if you want to take a close look at the famous St Oswald's, but by doing so, and exploring the Market Place on the way, you see the very best of the town.

Ashbourne Market Place, opposite the Town Hall, used to be lined with alehouses and, at one time, had its own bullring (close to the Wright Memorial, an elaborate piece of Victoriana). It was here that Bonnie Prince Charlie proclaimed his father King of England, and it was from here that the famous Shrovetide Football, between the 'Uppards' and 'Downards' of the town, always started. It was moved to Shaw Croft to reduce damage to property, but still rages along the Henmore, between the goals of Sturton Mill and Clifton Mill, each Easter. At the back of the Market Place is the Old Vaults pub, which used to be called The Anatomical Horse, with a skeleton for its sign. Down the narrow alley to the left is Victoria Square (once The Butchery and The Shambles) and Tiger Yard, beside a restaurant that used to be The Tiger Inn. The modern Victoria Square is a smart little suntrap, set about with benches.

Ashbourne's side streets and alleys are narrow and interesting; the layout of the old town north of the Henmore dates back to the 11th and 12th centuries and there are some fascinating nooks and crannies to explore, such as Lovatt's Yard and the House of Confinement (a lock-up) on Bellevue Street. However, it is along St John's Street and Church Street that the town's grandest buildings are to be found. Beyond the Clergy's Widows Almshouses are superb mansions and merchants' houses, several now serving as antiques shops, culminating in the magnificent stone-gabled Grammar School, founded by Elizabeth I in 1585. And opposite, set behind tall wrought-iron gates and a carpet of daffodils in the spring, stands St Oswald's. It was built around 1340 and perfectly described by the novelist George Eliot as 'the finest mere parish church in England'.

Insight

'OAKBOURNE'

Ashbourne is a perfect example of an English market town – eccentric street plan, narrow cobbled alleys, coaching inns, almshouses and market stalls. It needed very little alteration to become George Eliot's Oakbourne in *Adam Bede*, and is probably the best place in the Peak District to explore for antiques (but don't expect many bargains!).

CARSINGTON WATER

MAP REF SK2552

New reservoirs usually take years to blend with a landscape, and sometimes they never do. Carsington, opened by Her Majesty the Queen in 1992, already looks at home in the gently rolling hills southwest of Wirksworth.

Most of the Peak District's many reservoirs gather their water from acid moorland, so they are low in nutrients, and this in turn means they are poor for aquatic plants and animals. However, Carsington is quite different: it is filled largely by water pumped from rivers and so is excellent for wildlife. In the winter there are wildfowl by the thousand, including wigeon, pochard and tufted duck; in the summer there are great crested grebes and dabchicks; and in the spring and autumn, at migration time, all sorts of waders and seabirds use the reservoir as rest and refuelling stop on their arduous journeys.

A third of the Carsington shore is set aside as a conservation area, but the rest is accessible by footpath, by bicycle and by horse. The main Visitor Centre is on the west shore, with an extensive car park (pay-and-display) off the B5035.

There are several mining villages to the north of Carsington Water, including Brassington, which boasts some fine 18th-century houses and a Norman church. Inside the church, look for the even older carving high on the west wall of the tower of a naked man with his hands on his heart.

Hopton village is now dominated by the reservoir, though there is a bypass for the main road. Until 1989 Hopton Hall (not open) was the home of the Gell family, who made their fortune from the nearby limestone quarries, and made their name as scholars, politicians and travellers. Along the limestone rise to the north runs the Hopton Incline, once the steepest gradient for any standard-gauge railway line in Britain, using fixed engines and cable-haulage to set the High Peak Railway on its journey from Cromford Wharf to Whaley Bridge. It is now the High Peak Trail. Further north again is the Via Gellia, a road created and named by one of the Gells, through superb, flower-rich woodland along a valley west of Cromford.

Insight

THE RUDDY DUCK

One of Carsington Water's controversial residents is the American ruddy duck. Just 50 years ago this little duck (it has a big blue bill, white cheeks, a reddish back and a stiff tail) was quite unknown outside the Wildfowl Trust, but it escaped and is now so widespread that it is threatening to overrun Europe, diluting the genes of its close relative, the European white-headed duck, in the process.

Insight

NATURE RETURNED

Just north of Carsington and Hopton, the landscape rises to a 1,000-foot (305m) contour, topped by a stone called King's Chair. This area is pockmarked by old lead mines and limestone quarries, but wild flowers abound on the open limestone and into the Via Gellia; in places several kinds of orchid jostle for space, and in ash woodland there are patches of the rare herb *Paris quadrifolia*.

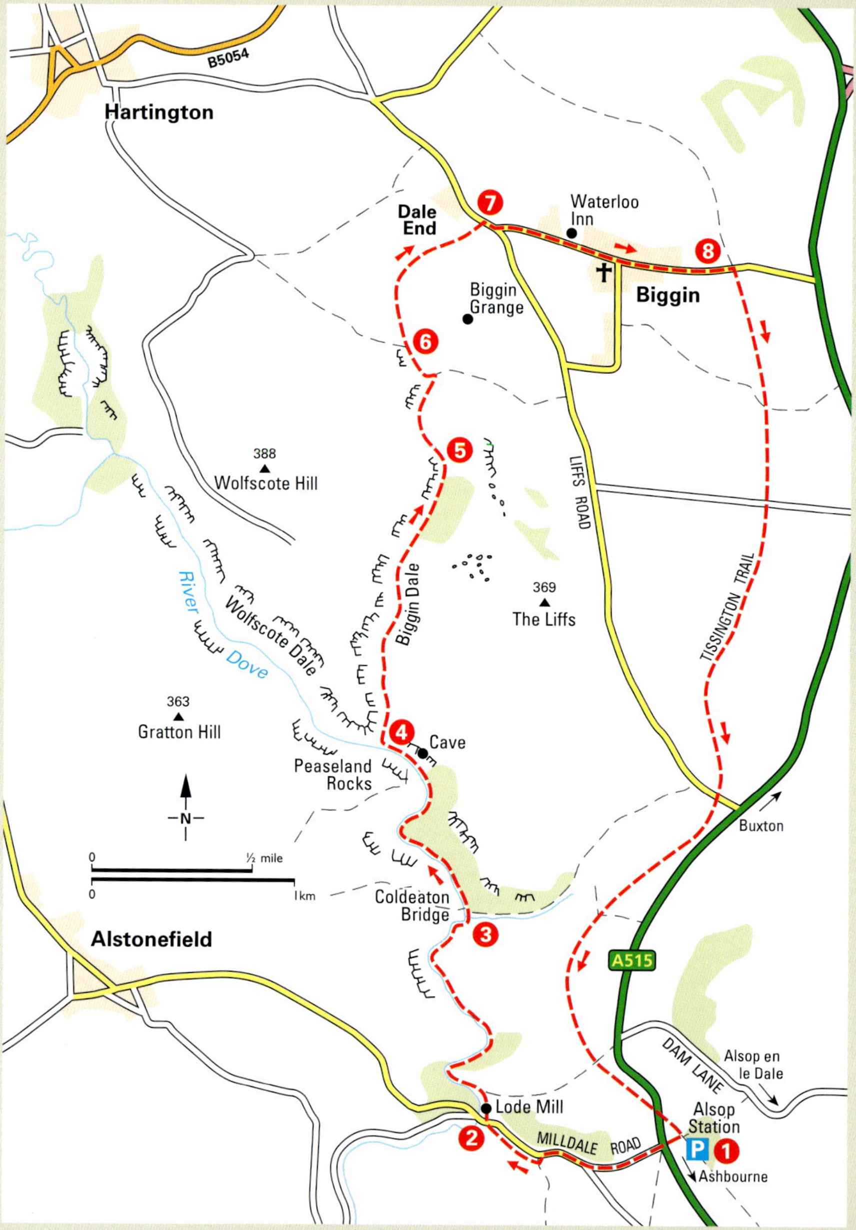
B5054
Hartington
Dale End
7
Waterloo Inn
8
Biggin Grange
Biggin
6
5
388
Wolfscote Hill
LIFFS ROAD
Biggin Dale
369
The Liffs
TISSINGTON TRAIL
River Dove
Wolfscote Dale
363
Gratton Hill
4
Cave
Peaseland Rocks
N
Buxton
0
½ mile
0
1km
Coldeaton Bridge
3
Alstonefield
A515
DAM LANE
Alsop en le Dale
Lode Mill
Alsop Station
2
MILLDALE ROAD
P
1
Ashbourne

Wolfscote and a Railway Trail

The first part of this very enjoyable walk winds through the scenic Wolfscote Dale and Biggin Dale, and you'll be walking through the heart of the upland limestone country. The return route is an easy-paced one, using the Tissington Trail, which ambles quietly over the high pastures of Biggin and Alsop moors.

Route facts

DISTANCE/TIME 7.5 miles (12.1km) 5h

MAP OS Explorer OL24 White Peak

START Tissington Trail pay car park near Alsop en le Dale, grid ref SK 156549

TRACKS Well-defined paths, several stiles

GETTING TO THE START
The walk begins at Alsop Old Station, one of the former station sites on the Tissington Trail. It is signposted off the A515 about 6 miles (9.7km) north of Ashbourne.

THE PUB The Waterloo Inn, Biggin-by-Hartington. Tel: 01298 84284

! The limestone dale sides can be slippery after rain.

Route Directions

1 From the car park at the former Alsop Station, cross the busy A515 and follow the Milldale Road immediately opposite. After a junction you are offered a parallel footpath on the left, keeping you safe from the traffic.

2 On reaching the bottom of the dale by Lode Mill, turn right along the footpath, tracing the river's east bank through a winding, partially wooded valley.

3 Ignore the footpath on the right at Coldeaton Bridge, but instead stay with Wolfscote Dale beneath thickly wooded slopes on the right. Beyond a stile the woods cease and the dale becomes bare and rock-fringed, with a cave on the right and the bold pinnacles of Peaseland Rocks ahead. Here the valley sides open out into the dry valley of Biggin Dale, where this route goes next.

4 The signposted path into Biggin Dale begins beyond a gate in a cross-wall and follows that wall. It continues through scrub woodland and beneath limestone screes. Beyond a gate you enter a nature reserve.

5 There is another gate at the far end of the nature reserve. Beyond the gate, the dale curves left, then right, before dividing again beneath the hill pastures of Biggin Grange. Divert left here, through a gate to follow the footpath, signposted to Hartington. On the other side of the wall there is a concrete dewpond.

6 After 200yds (183m) you'll reach another junction of paths. Ignore the one signposted to Hartington and keep walking ahead up the shallowing dale, following the path for Biggin. It stays with the valley round to the right, passing a small sewage works (left) before climbing out of the dale to reach the road at Dale End.

7 Turn right along the road for a few paces then left, following a road past the Waterloo Inn and through Biggin village.

8 On the far side of the former railway bridge towards the top of the hill join the Tissington Trail bridleway. Follow this old trackbed southwards, across the pastures of Biggin and Alport moors, for 2 miles (3.2km) until you reach the car park.

The Staffordshire Moorlands

An undulating, on-road route through the countryside where the White Peak and Dark Peak meet, visiting Longnor, 'Cardale' in the TV series *Peak Practice*.

Route Directions

1 Take the short steep climb up the B5054 road outside The Manifold Inn to a junction on the left signposted 'Sheen & Longnor'. This winding lane initially descends before starting a gradual climb between limestone walls. Sight lines on this section are not good, but they improve after a slightly steeper pitch brings the route to the straggling village of Sheen.

2 The road undulates through the village, with good views to the higher Staffordshire moorlands. Passing by the village inn, The Staffordshire Knot, then the church, the way again steepens slightly as it rises through a few bends to level out past Harris Close farm, with Sheen Hill's rugged top drawing the eye left. A long, easy ride follows, cresting to fall down a fairly short, sharp hill with bad sight lines. At the junction keep ahead to reach Longnor; from this short section are views across to the hamlet of Crowdecote and up the Dove to the sharp peaks of Chrome and Parkhouse hills.

3 At the heart of Longnor is the Market Square. This route crosses straight over the junction here, in front of The Horseshoe pub and along a lane signposted 'Royal Cottage and Leek'. Once out of the village there's a steep descent to a bridge over the River Manifold, heralding the start of a long steady climb up the valley side. On the right is the old village sawmill, now transformed into apartments. In 0.5 mile (800m) the route levels along a long, tree-lined straight to reach a left turn signposted 'Fawfieldhead and Newtown'. Follow this through to a T-junction and turn right along an undulating lane with pleasing views.

4 At a telephone box turn left along a lane signposted 'Warslow'. Soon you'll pass by the little chapel at Newtown (built 1837) off to your right in its overgrown churchyard. This is an airy, easy cruise along a high road, with the distinctive limestone hills at Ecton the main feature off to your left beyond Reaps Moor. Beyond a house called Hayshead the lane starts a long, gradual climb before levelling out beside Lum Edge and Warslow Moor.

Route facts

DISTANCE/TIME 13 miles (21km) 3h30

MAP OS Explorer OL24 White Peak

START The Manifold Inn, grid ref SK 106593

TRACKS All on-road apart from a short section of the Manifold Trail at the end

GETTING TO THE START Hulme End is on the B5054 west of Hartington. Ask at The Manifold Inn if you can park and ride. Alternatively, cross the river bridge and drive to the pay car park at the Manifold Valley Visitor Centre at Hulme End, then cycle to The Manifold Inn.

CYCLE HIRE Parsley Hay on the High Peak Trail, 4 miles (6.4km) from Hulme End. Tel: 01298 84493

THE PUB The Manifold Inn, Hulme End. Tel: 01298 84537; www.themanifoldinn.co.uk

❗ Take care on the short sections of busier road at the start, just beyond Longnor, before Warslow and the very short section of B-road at Warslow. Suitable for older children with on-road cycling experience and not averse to the odd challenging hill climb.

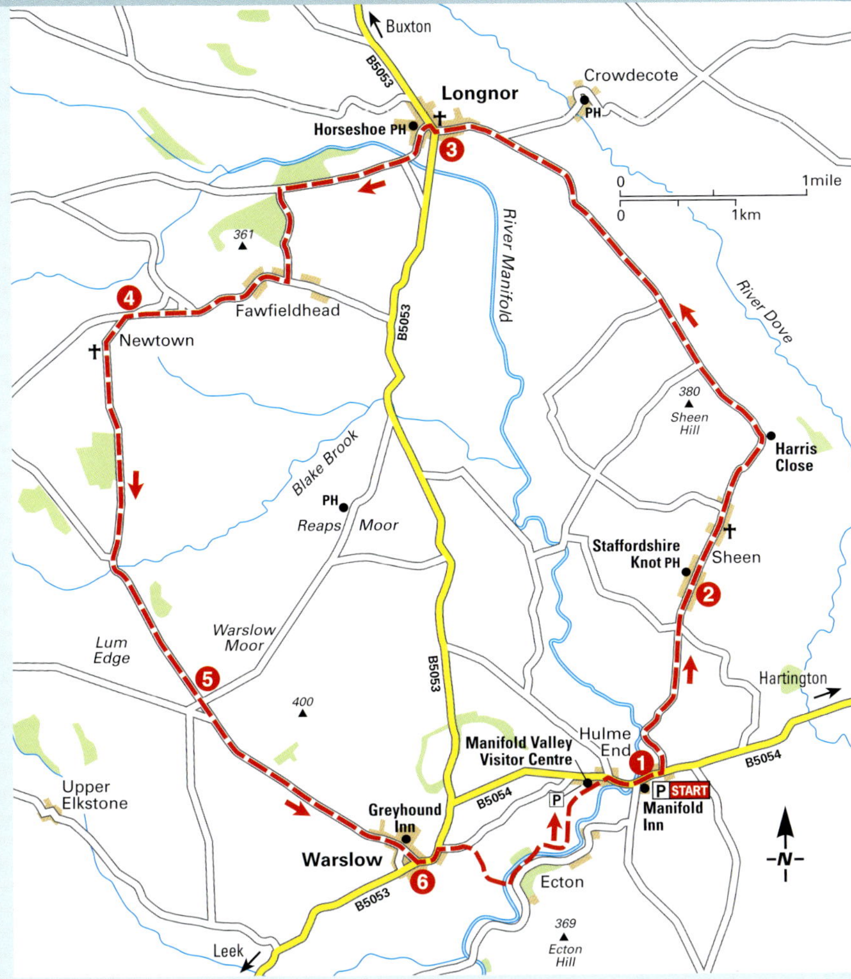

5 Go straight across the crossroads, bear left at the junction, joining a road that rises gradually, soon crossing a cattle grid. Cresting another rise, there's a long descent into Warslow. Continue to pass the Greyhound Inn to a junction with the B5053.

6 Turn left along this road and remain on it for about 200yds (183m) to find a lane on the right, signposted 'Unsuitable for Heavy Goods Vehicles'. Carefully turn into this, which drops increasingly steeply as a narrow, winding lane. Keep right to descend to a bridge across the Manifold. Just beyond this turn left along the Manifold Way and follow this to Hulme End. Rejoin the main road and turn right to return to the nearby Manifold Inn and the start of the ride.

DOVEDALE MAP REF SK1551

Fame, beauty and availability are a heady mix. Dovedale's Stepping Stones appear on a thousand postcards and attract a million visitors, all of whom seem to be queuing to cross the crystal waters of the Dove at the same time. The National Trust does a heroic job to manage this part of its South Peak Estate, but it is perhaps a good idea to keep away from the place on sunny Sundays.

The Dove flows for 45 miles (72.4km), but only a short section of it is called Dovedale; above the Viator Bridge it becomes Mill Dale, then Wolfscote Dale and then Beresford Dale. But it is to the gorge of Dovedale that the visitors flock, for within the space of a few miles of easy riverside walking, on a broad level path, there are superb craggy rocks and pillars (all named) rising out of dense ash woodland, sweeps of open pasture, banks of flowers, dark caves and fine cascades of spring water.

There is no road, and only one main path, following the east (Derbyshire) bank. It is not even necessary to cross the stepping stones upstream from the car park on the Staffordshire side of the river, because there is a footbridge a few yards away.

Victorian fashion blighted Dovedale; it was praised by every famous romantic writer from Byron to Tennyson and was soon as popular as Switzerland. Donkey tours and guided expeditions once ferried people up the path to view the scenery. Of more enduring merit were the earlier words of Izaak Walton, who loved the Dove and put his head and heart into *The Compleat Angler*.

HARTINGTON MAP REF SK1260

Hartington is a tourist honeypot but, like Tissington and Ashford, there is enough in the fabric and culture of the village to cope with popularity and still have a heart. Curiously, its heart is probably the duck pond, or mere, which sits like a round pearl in a circlet of duck-cropped lawn. Nearby is Ye Olde Cheese Shoppe, selling superb local Dovedale Blue. Just a stone's-throw away are tea rooms, shops, a pottery and two pubs – old coaching inns from the days when Hartington was a significant market town. One has the unusual name, The Charles Cotton, after the angling resident of Beresford Hall, friend and collaborator of Izaak Walton. It was on the upper reaches of the Dove as it flowed below Beresford Hall that Cotton and Walton perfected their arts and gathered their fishing stories, published in 1653 as *The Compleat Angler*.

Just out of the village, up a steep side road to the east, is Hartington Hall, a sturdy yeoman's manor built in the 17th century. It was the home of the Bateman family but has been a youth hostel since 1934. Also to the east of the village is a signal box of the Ashbourne–Buxton Railway, which closed in 1967 and is now an information centre on the Tissington Trail, while 3 miles (4.8km) north is Pilsbury Castle, now a mound, probably on the site of an Iron Age fort.

Hartington occupies a strategic position for walkers and explorers of the less obvious paths and byways. To the east and the west lie dry valleys and a lattice of green pastures and to the south is Beresford Dale.

ILAM MAP REF SK1350

On most maps the River Manifold can be traced in a blue line, flowing south from Longnor to meet the Dove 1 mile (1.6km) below Ilam. In fact this is not usually what happens, and, like several other celebrated rivers in limestone country, the Manifold has a secret life, flowing underground unless the water table is high. Below Wettonmill the river abruptly disappears and takes almost 24 hours to resurface, at the Boil Holes in the grounds of Ilam Hall. This explains why there are no footpaths along what appears on paper to be a pretty section of the lower valley. This does not mean the landscape is not interesting, but there is no clear focal point, and the footpaths linking to the old halls of Throwley and Castern on the upper slopes of the valley are rarely walked.

Ilam, above the confluence of two famous rivers, has always been an important settlement, but never very large. Originally it belonged to Burton Abbey, but after the Reformation the estate was broken up among three families, the Ports of Ilam Hall, the Meverells of Throwley and the Hurts of Castern. Of these the Meverells no longer exist and Throwley Hall is a ruin; the Ports sold Ilam to Jesse Watts Russell in the early 19th century, and the Hurts still live at secluded Castern.

Alas, Russell swept away most of old Ilam and built a model village, the buildings of which have the look of a Swiss cuckoo clock. Ilam Hall was rebuilt on a grand scale; a quarter of it remains and is used as a youth hostel. The lovely parkland that surrounds it is open to the public. Close by is the church, totally rebuilt, but with two fragments from Saxon crosses and a Tudor chapel with a shrine to the local medieval hermit St Bertram.

The Ilam estate passed to the care of the National Trust in 1934 and is a popular destination for day visitors, partly because of its pleasant walks and partly because it is close to Dovedale and has literary associations – with Boswell, Johnson and Izaak Walton.

Insight

MAGNIFICENT MANIFOLD

Cyclists and ramblers following the Manifold Trail are passing through some of the best ash woods anywhere in Europe. Clothing the gorge-sides in their feathery foliage, the woodlands provide a home for a remarkable assemblage of wildlife; more than 240 plant and 150 insect types are present, together with dozens of bird species drawn by this natural bounty; summer evenings find bats skimming the river's languid pools and fragrant meadows for bugs and moths.

LONGNOR MAP REF SK0864

The fate of little Longnor was sealed by the demise of the turnpikes and the lack of a railway link; its worthy ambition to be a proper market town withered away. It stands now in the no man's land that lies between the Manifold and the Dove, but at a pivotal point in the Peak District, in the very heart of the country. Around it lie strip fields dating back to medieval times; just to the north lies Derbyshire and the limestone knoll country, while to the west are the darker gritstone hills of Staffordshire.

The Manifold at Longnor is no more than a babbling brook, but the valley is broad, with meadows and sandstone barns. Yellowhammers and whitethroats sing from the thorn bushes; swallows swoop for insects over the reed-grass. Longnor presides over the long, straight road like a drowsy cat over a barn floor. The village is pretty and compact, with a little square and a Victorian market hall. A stone inscription above the entrance carries the tariff of ancient market tolls.

MANIFOLD VALLEY

MAP REF SK0956

The Manifold and the Dove rise within a mile of each other below Axe Edge. As they head southeast together into limestone country, twisting and side-winding like pulled strands of wool, one is transmuted into a Staffordshire valley, the other into a Derbyshire dale. The difference in landscape terms is quite minimal; they both cut a course through superb scenery, meeting finally at Ilam, yet the Manifold Valley escaped all the Victorian hype and the more carnival atmosphere of Dovedale.

Wetton and Warslow villages, on the 1,000-foot (305m) contour on opposite sides of the valley, are the main access points for the most dramatic section of the Manifold. Neither makes very much concession to tourists, though both have good pubs (the Olde Royal Oak and the Greyhound). Warslow has a utilitarian look, as do its medieval iron stocks close to the school. It is an estate village of the Crewe family (of Calke Abbey, south of Derby) and lies at the very foot of the gritstone moors, which can be reached by taking the side road to the northwest. Wetton is on the limestone, among dairy farms and barns, but its stout church and many of its cottages look as if they belong amongst heather.

A steep side road north of Warslow off the B5053 drops down to Ecton, and the most beautiful section of the valley begins. It runs southwards along a thin strip of level meadow, with steep, flower-studded, almost alpine-looking, grassland on either side. The road, and what is now the Manifold Trail, follows the route of the Leek and Manifold Valley Light Railway, which opened in 1904 but only survived for 30 years; according to expert judgement it opened too late and closed too soon – if its odd Indian-style engines were still running today the line would make a fortune!

Close by to Wettonmill the Manifold usually disappears down swallow-holes, travelling all the rest of the way to Ilam underground. Meanwhile, the Manifold's tributary, the Hamps, heads southwards and the Manifold Trail stays with the old railway line, going along the Hamps to the large village of Waterhouses.

Once out of the depth of the valley, the steep limestone hill slopes are pockmarked with deep caves. The most famous and dramatic is Thor's Cave but several others, such as Ossom's Cave and Elderbush, have been explored or excavated and have produced bones and flints from the Stone and Bronze Ages, when this was good hunting country. All the domed hills, which are called Lows, are capped by cairns or barrows and it is very easy on the dry 'karst' hillsides to imagine yourself in another older world.

BUTCHERY

Insight & Visit

WELL DRESSING

The most famous and picturesque of all the Peak District traditions, well dressing, probably has its roots in pagan ceremonies to placate water spirits, but the Christian version has its origins at Tissington, where the five wells ran with pure water through the years of the Black Death. The villagers believed they owed their lives to the water, and dressed the tops of the wells as a sign of thanksgiving. Well dressing involves pressing flower petals, cones, seeds and fruits onto a clay base to create a picture, often of a Biblical or local scene. Well dressings take place throughout the late spring and summer.

Activity

THE TISSINGTON TRAIL

The famous Tissington Trail runs for 13 miles (20.9km) from Parsley Hay to Ashbourne, along the old railway line which closed in 1963. You will find that the trail is particularly suitable for families and cyclists who appreciate a car-free countryside; it is possible to hire bikes at either Parsley Hay or Ashbourne, or bring your own and leave your car at the car park, on the site of the old railway station.

TISSINGTON MAP REF SK1752

Tissington is a gem, too beautiful for its own good on summer Sundays but a gift to any photographer. The classic approach is off the A515, through a gateway and over a cattle grid, then along a drive lined with lime trees. The original avenue, of venerable pollards and tall standards, has recently been felled, but there are rows of young trees set further back. Into the village itself, past a walled yew and the first of several wells, sandstone cottages are set back behind wide grass verges and shaded by elegant beeches. There is a village green, with the stream running through it, a duck pond complete with ducks, a Norman church and a grand Jacobean Hall. This is, and has been for centuries, an idyllic, well-managed estate village.

Tissington Hall, low and wide with mullioned windows and tall chimneys, is the home of the Fitzherbert family. It is set behind a low wall and gate of fine wrought ironwork (by Robert Bakewell).

The overwhelming impression of Tissington is of its perfect blend of old stone houses, trees and water. Every wall is draped in flowers and creepers. A few decades ago there would have been the sound of steam trains, but the line closed in 1963 and the trackway is now a walk/cycle/horse-riding route, managed by the National Park Authority and known as the Tissington Trail.

A few miles southwest along the Tissington Trail, beside the A515, is the village of Fenny Bentley. The village is dominated by a square 15th-century tower, incorporated into the more recent Cherry Orchard Farm. The tower was part of the old Hall, the home of the Beresford family, and in St Edmund's Church is an alabaster tomb to Thomas Beresford and his family. Thomas fought at Agincourt with eight of his sons; these, together with his wife and their further 14 children, are depicted on and around the tomb as bodies wrapped in shrouds, probably because by the time the tomb was built nobody would have known what they had looked like.

WIRKSWORTH MAP REF SK2854

A few years ago Wirksworth was a town of quarry dust and fusty alleys, growing old disgracefully. Now it is one of the most fascinating places to visit in the area, full of history, neat and welcoming. This shows what can happen with a little vision and civic enthusiasm, but there is a suspicion that the hard edges of Wirksworth's past, as a lead-mining and quarrying centre, have been smoothed away rather than dusted off. The lead mining industry disappeared many years ago, to be replaced by quarrying, which is still of considerable local importance. The National Stone Centre just outside the town gives a fuller picture of this southeast corner of the Peak. Nearby is the old quarry of Black Rock, a picnic spot with a 4-mile (6.4km) forest trail over Cromford Moor and access to the High Peak Trail (the old railway line that once transported stone to the Cromford Canal).

The heart of Wirksworth is the Market Place and car park, from where it is possible to explore the town in several directions. Up Dale End there are wickedly sloping lanes with cobbled gutters, leading past the old smithy, opposite Green Hill, a fine 17th-century gabled house built of limestone with sandstone mullioned windows. Further up the hill is Babington House (not open), of similar vintage, set in a pretty garden and with a fine view over the town. It is a three-storey residence, with a stone sundial on the gable wall.

South from the Market Place, past the Town Hall, is Coldwell Street with several old inns, including The Red Lion, The Vaults, which were originally called The Compleat Angler, and The George. Down Chapel Lane is Moot Hall (not open), the only place in England where lead-miners' Barmote Courts (to settle any lead-mining disputes) are still held (they started here in 1266, though this building only dates back to 1814). Inside there is a Miners Standard Dish, dated 1513, which was used for measuring the ore, as a levy had to be paid to both the King and the Barmaster who was in charge of the court. The Barmote Court still sits each April.

Hidden away behind the fronts of tall houses is St Mary's Church. It is accessible along Church Street or through the old alley of the lychgate, of which only the tall stone pillars remain. The grassed churchyard is encircled by iron railings, which separate it from a narrow lane called Church Walk, and an engaging jumble of back yards and sloping roofs. The church itself is broad and solid with an eccentrically tiny spire or spike, as if all but the top few feet had fallen through the roof of the tower.

Visit

THE VIRGIN AND THE GYPSY

Middleton lies on the brow of the hill just north of Wirksworth and there are excellent long views across the valley of the Via Gellia. The author D H Lawrence lived here for a year and the village featured as 'Woodlinkin' in his novella *The Virgin and the Gypsy*. Near by is Middleton Top, a main access and bike-hire station onto the High Peak Trail.

■ TOURIST INFORMATION CENTRE

Ashbourne
13 The Market Place.
Tel: 01335 343666

Hulme End
Manifold Valley Visitor Centre.
Tel: 01298 84679 (seasonal)

■ PLACES OF INTEREST

Derwent Crystal
Shawcroft, Ashbourne.
Tel: 01335 345219;
www.derwentcrystal.co.uk

Ecclesbourne Valley Railway
Wirksworth Station.
Tel: 01629 823076; www.ecclesbournevalleyrailway.org.uk

High Peak Junction Workshops
Wirksworth.
Tel: 01629 822831. Original workshops, railway exhibition and information centre.

Ilam Park
4.5 miles (7.2km) northwest of Ashbourne. Woods and parkland on the banks of the River Manifold. Free but parking fees apply.

Middleton Top Engine House
Middleton Top Visitor Centre, Middleton by Wirksworth.
Tel: 01629 823204
Engine house with a beam engine to haul wagons up the Middleton incline.

National Stone Centre
Porter Lane, Wirksworth.
Tel: 01629 825403; www.nationalstonecentre.org.uk.
Exhibition, guided walks and gem panning.

Steeple Grange Light Railway
The Quarry Men's Line, Middleton by Wirksworth.
Tel: 01246 205542;
www.steeplegrange.co.uk
Rides every ten minutes.

Wirksworth Heritage Centre
Crown Yard.
Tel: 01629 825225; www.storyofwirksworth.co.uk
Former silk and velvet mill with displays illustrating the town's history.

■ SHOPPING

Ashbourne
Antiques shops in Church Street.
General market, Thu and Sat.

Wirksworth
General market, Tue.

■ LOCAL SPECIALITIES

Cheeses
Derbyshire and Staffordshire cheeses (and bottled beers) from Ye Olde Cheese Shoppe, Hartington.
Tel: 01298 84935;
www.hartingtoncheese.co.uk

Crafts
Longnor Craft Centre, The Market Hall, Longnor.
Tel: 01298 83587

Honey
Daisybank Apiaries, Newtown, Longnor.
Tel: 01298 83526;
www.daisybankapiaries.co.uk
Peak District honey, mead.

Pottery
Rooke's, 1 Mill Lane, Hartington.
Tel: 01298 84650;
www.rookespottery.co.uk

■ SPORTS & ACTIVITIES

ANGLING

Fly Fishing
Carsington Water.
Tel: 01629 540478;
www.stwater.co.uk

BOAT HIRE
Carsington Water.
Tel: 01629 540478;
www.stwater.co.uk

CYCLING *see* LONG-DISTANCE FOOTPATHS AND TRAILS

CYCLE HIRE
(For those marked P, website is www.peakdistrict.gov.uk)

Ashbourne (P)
Ashbourne Cycle Hire Centre, Mapleton Lane.
Tel: 01335 343156

Carsington Water
Tel: 01629 540478;
www.stwater.co.uk

Middleton Top (P)
Visitor Centre, Middleton by Wirksworth.
Tel: 01629 823204

Parsley Hay (P)
Peak District National Park Centre, Waterhouses.
Tel: 01298 84493

Brown End Farm Cycle Hire
Brown End Farm.
Tel: 01538 308313;
www.manifoldcycling-brownendarm.co.uk

Manifold Valley Bike Hire
Earls Way, Old Station Car Park. Tel: 01538 308609;
www.visitpeakdistrict.com

GUIDED WALKS

Derbyshire Dales Countryside Service
Planning and Development Services, Town Hall, Matlock. Full guided walks service.
Tel: 01629 761326

National Park Walks with a Ranger
Peak District National Park.
Tel: 01629 816200;
www.peakdistrict.gov.uk

Peak District
Annual Peak District Walking Festival. Guided walks April/May. Tel: 0870 444 7275;
www.visitpeakdistrict.com/activities/walking

Wirksworth & Peak District
Professional Blue Badge Guides. Tel: 01629 534284

HANG-GLIDING

Airways Airsports
Ashbourne.
Tel: 01335 344308;
www.airways-airsports.com

HORSE-RIDING

Tissington Trekking Centre,
Tissington Wood Farm, Ashbourne. Tel: 01335 350276

LONG-DISTANCE FOOTPATHS AND TRAILS

The High Peak Trail
Follows the former High Peak Railway from High Peak Junction (Cromford) to Dowlow (south of Buxton). Derbyshire Countryside Centre. Tel: 01629 823204

Manifold Trail
Traces a former narrow-gauge railway from Hulme End to Waterhouses, 8.25 miles (13.3km) of walking or cycling. Visitor Centre at Hulme End.

The Tissington Trail
Part of old Ashbourne–Buxton railway. Runs for 13 miles (21km) alongside Dovedale from Ashbourne, and joins the High Peak Trail near Parsley Hay. Derbyshire Countryside Centre.
Tel: 01629 823204

WATERSPORTS

Carsington Water
Near Ashbourne.
Tel: 01629 540478

■ ANNUAL EVENTS & CUSTOMS

For the full programme visit www.visitpeakdistrict.com

Ashbourne
Shrovetide Football, Shrove Tue–Ash Wed.
Highland Gathering, with parade of pipe bands, mid-Jul.
Ashbourne Show, late Aug.
Well dressing (Wyaston & Mayfield), mid-Jun

Bonsall
Hen racing, The Barley Mow pub, early Aug.
Well-dressing, Jul.

Dovedale
The Dovedale Dash, a 4.25-mile (6.8km) cross-country run which starts on Thorpe Pastures, early Nov.

Hartington
Well dressing, Sep.

Ilam
Manifold Valley Agricultural Show, The Arbour, Castern Hall Farm, early Aug.
Dovedale Sheepdog Trials, mid-Aug.

Longnor
Well dressing and Wakes, early Sep.
Longnor Races, Sep.

Tissington
Well dressing, Ascension Day.
World Toe-Wrestling Championships, (Bentley Brook Inn), Jun.

Wirksworth
Well dressing, late May.
Clypping of the Church service, early Sep.
Festival of Music and Arts, Sep.

■ DOVEDALE

Tea Rooms

Bassett Wood Farm

Tissington, Ashbourne, Derbyshire DE6 1RD Tel: 01335 350254; www.bassettwoodfarm.co.uk

This friendly, welcoming and informal tea room set in a working farmhouse is always heady with the rich aroma of home-baking. Look out for local jams, honey and dairy produce and indulge in tasty ice-creams.

Beresford Tea Room

Market Place, Hartington, Derbyshire SK17 0AL Tel: 01298 84418

This tea room is also the village post office. As ever, local produce and local baking is to the fore; try some of the local Dovedale Blue (maybe on a chilli oatcake). In the winter months, the hotpot is particularly welcoming.

Manifold Tearooms

Ilam Hall, Ilam, Staffordshire DE6 2AZ. Tel: 01335 350245

The stable block to the Hall (a youth hostel) is now a National Trust tea room with an emphasis on vegetarian and organic foods. Enjoy tea and cakes or try one of the more substantial meals. The local cheeses are also good.

Craft Centre Coffee Shop

Longnor Market Hall, Longnor, Staffordshire SK17 0N. Tel: 01298 83587

This enterprising little café serves a variety of home baked produce including Staffordshire oatcakes. The little Victorian Market Hall is also home to locally made art and crafts, all for sale.

Pubs

The Yew Tree Inn

Cauldon, Waterhouses, Staffordshire ST10 3EJ Tel: 01538 308348

Antiques, furniture and bric-a-brac fill the warren of rooms behind the lattice windows of this magical old pub. You'll find real ales though food is limited to pies, baps and sandwiches. Don't let the quarry dust put you off – this one is a real winner.

Ye Olde Gate Inn

Well Street, Brassington, Derbyshire DE4 4HJ Tel: 01629 540228

This is a tremendous old pub – haunted of course – with low, dark beams (salvaged from an Armada ship), old blackened ranges, quarry-tile floors, old settles and pews and a superbly atmospheric snug. There's also grand local fodder and several real ales to enjoy.

The Pack Horse Inn

Crowdecote, near Buxton, Derbyshire SK17 0DB Tel: 01298 83618

Set in a tiny hamlet above the upper Dove Valley, with small simply furnished rooms sitting beneath a higgledy-piggledy roof. Enjoy the fine quality food menu and beers from local microbreweries in the raised beer-garden.

The Barley Mow

The Dale, Bonsall, Cromford, Derbyshire DE4 2AY Tel: 01629 825685; www. barleymowbonsall.co.uk

The friendly landlord tells tales of UFOs, ghosts and ghouls at this old village pub, with its warm winter fires, grand, home-cooked food, locally brewed beers and an unspoiled interior.

The George Inn

Alstonefield, Ashbourne, Staffordshire DE6 2FX Tel: 01335 3102; www. thegeorgealstonefield.com

The George has beamed rooms, quarry-tile floors and log fires, old photos and polished plate. You'll find filling, home-made pub food and a couple of real ales from regional breweries. In summer, sit in the cool courtyard beneath an immense ash tree.

THE GOYT VALLEY

Buxton & Western Moors

Macclesfield and Leek mark the western and southern edges of the Peak uplands: to the north are Whaley Bridge and Chapel-en-le-Frith. In-between are dramatic gritstone outcrops and windswept heather moors. Two rivers drain the watershed: to the north the Goyt, rising on the peaty slopes of the Cat and Fiddle Moor; to the south the pretty River Dane. To the east of all this is the grand spa town of Buxton.

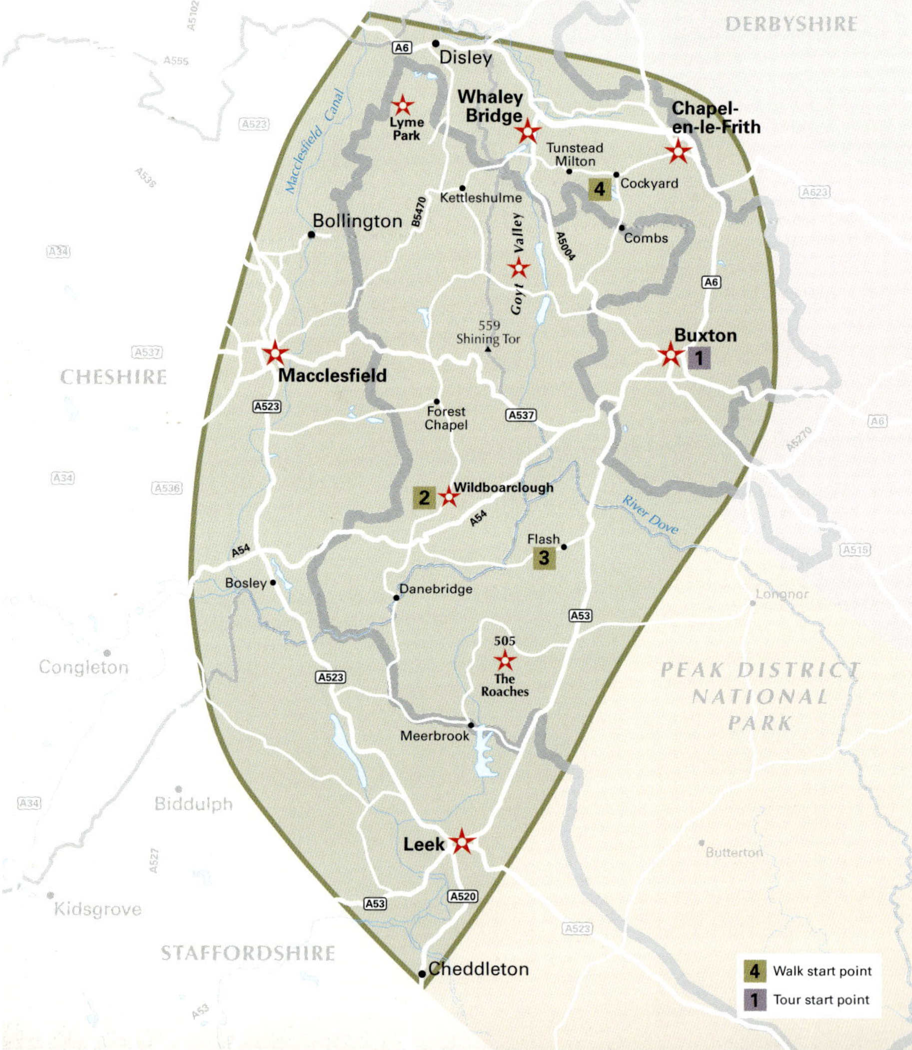

THE GOYT VALLEY

THE ROACHES

Unmissable attractions

Leek, which was built on the silk industry, is where the first hills of the Peak District rise up from the Staffordshire Plain. These heights are known as the Staffordshire Moorlands and are marked by outcrops, such as the Roaches and neighbouring Ramshaw Rocks and Hen Cloud. Unsurprisingly, they are very popular with hang gliders and rock climbers. By contrast, the elegant spa town of Buxton lies at the centre of the Peak. Its many buildings of note include the Royal Crescent and the Opera House. Opposite the Crescent is St Ann's Well, the source of Buxton's famous heated spa water and nearby is the awesome gulf of Poole's Cavern, the Peak's most accessible cave for intrepid explorers.

2

3

4

1 Erwood Reservoir, Goyt Valley
It looks as if it has always been here, but Errwood Reservoir is a relatively recent addition to the valley landscape, along with its neighbour Fernilee. Built by Stockport Corporation, Fernilee was flooded in 1938 and Errwood followed in 1967. The Forestry Commission added woodlands in the 1960s. A fly-fishing club and a sailing club both make use of Errwood Reservoir.

2 The Roaches
The magnificent tilted ridge of The Roaches, stands with Hen Cloud beyond. This dramatic millstone grit outcrop is famous for rock climbing and for its feral population of wallabies.

3 Buxton
Situated in the Pavilion Gardens, on the banks of the River Wye, the impressive domed Octagon was first opened to the public in 1876. This magnificent glass and cast-iron structure today operates as a concert venue and also hosts antiques and collectors' fairs.

4 Whaley Bridge
The Peak Forest Canal ends at the picturesque Whaley Bridge canal basin. Colourful narrowboats and the tow path both provide a more leisurely way to explore this beautiful area.

BUXTON MAP REF SK0573

Dropping down from the high moors into the elegant spa town of Buxton, on the River Wye, is enough to make anyone blink in disbelief as they find themselves emerging out of the bleak wilderness into a bower of parks and gardens and grand Palladian-style buildings.

Through the centuries health resorts have sprung up in all sorts of unlikely places, and none more so than Buxton. The Romans, who had a passion for bathing, established a rest or leisure facility here in the days of Agricola, when the frontier fighting had shifted north to Caledonia and this was a safe haven with the additional benefit of natural warm springs. After the Romans left, the Christians came to take the 'cripple's cure' at St Ann's Well and to pray for miracles.

By the 18th century Buxton, in common with other spa towns, was set firmly on the fashion trail. The 5th Duke of Devonshire was responsible for the main wave of building innovation at Buxton. He had been impressed in the 1770s by the Royal Crescent at Bath and was awash with money from his Ecton copper mines. First he had the elegant semicircular Crescent built, complete with 42 pilasters and 378 windows, then the Great Stable with a central court and Tuscan columns, finally followed by Hall Bank and The Square, all built in a grand and imposing style.

In the 19th century the 6th and 7th Dukes carried on the work, so that by late Victorian times the spa in the valley had completely eclipsed the old market town on the upper slope. The Great Stable became the Devonshire Hospital, 'for the use of the sick poor', and was given a massive domed roof 156 feet (47.5m) across (it is now part of The University of Derby); terraces of hotels and guest houses sprang up to cater for the influx of affluent visitors to the Thermal and Natural Baths; the railways arrived, the beautiful Pavilion Gardens were laid out on the banks of the Wye, and in 1905 the magnificent Opera House was opened.

Surprisingly, the majority of Buxton's fine buildings are still functioning and thriving. The Edwardian Opera House has a full programme, taking advantage of the current interest in opera. Outside is an immaculate square, complete with an ornate Victorian post box, and behind it run the Pavilion Gardens, complete with a Serpentine Walk.

Perhaps the best way to soak up the town's authentic atmosphere is to park your car at the market place in the old town (it vies with Alston in Cumbria in its claim to be the highest market town in England) and walk past the town hall, down a path across the grassy dome called The Slopes towards the Crescent. Few places in England evoke such a comfortable, Pre-Raphaelite sense of town and country. Plenty of shopping

Insight

THE BEST BREW

Local people still queue up at St Ann's Well in Buxton to fill plastic containers with the tepid water, claiming it makes the best tea in Britain. Try it straight from the well. It was good enough for Mary, Queen of Scots, and it was water that brought the Romans into the Peak District in the first place.

arcades keep the streets lively and local businesses thriving. There are weekly markets and you will find the Tourist Information Centre on the site of the original mineral baths. Opposite The Crescent is the famous twin-domed old Pump Room, where smart visitors once took their prescribed mineral waters. Nearby stands a modest fountain, which is the source of the famous waters and of Buxton's continued prosperity.

CHAPEL-EN-LE-FRITH

MAP REF SK0580

Unfortunately, a pretty name does not always describe a picturesque place. The frith, or forest, never really existed except to formalise a vast tract of Norman hunting preserve; most of the Derbyshire countryside was open ground rather than woodland.

The most obvious feature of Chapel-en-le-Frith today is its rather dowdy main road, which sweeps south into a hollow and on towards Buxton. A bypass now carries A6 traffic around to the east, but it will take some years for this part of Chapel to brighten up. However, turning off the main road at the white-painted Kings Arms at the top of the town, brings you directly to the market place and a change of character. Lovely cobbled paths and a medieval cross and stocks stand at the heart of the little square, overlooked by a café called The Stocks. Except on market day (Thursday) this is a quiet and out of the way place, perfect for a cup of tea and a wander. Close by is the Roebuck Inn, and a little way further along the street, opposite the church, is what was once the Bull's Head Inn, of which only the sign, a wooden carved life-size shorthorn bull's head, still survives.

St Thomas à Becket Church stands on a grassy knoll overlooking a housing estate. The original chapel in the forest was built here around 1225, but was replaced in the early 14th century by a sturdier structure. Most of what is visible today is from the refurbishment of 1733, but there are hints of antiquity all around; the shaft of a Saxon cross, a weathered sundial, and a view across what must have been glorious hunting country to the scenic crag-fringed edges of Combs Moss.

Insight

HEATHER ON THE MOORS

Common heather, or ling, turns the moors purple in August, but there are two other kinds of heather on the hills around Buxton – cross-leaved heather found on wet or boggy ground and bell-heather found on dry, rocky slopes. Both these plants have bigger flowers than the common heather, but don't attract as many bees. Heather honey is a local speciality.

Insight

BRUTAL TIMES

One morbid episode in Chapel's history casts a long shadow. In the Civil War, following the Battle of Ribbleton Moor in 1648, 1,500 Scottish soldiers were imprisoned in the church for 16 days. The conditions must have been appalling. By the time they were let out, to start a forced march north, 44 men were dead. They were buried in the churchyard, a testament to brutal times.

The village of Combs, just southwest of Chapel-en-le-Frith, has stone-built cottages centred on the welcoming Beehive Inn. A short walk away is Combs Reservoir, which has a sailing club and is also a popular spot for coarse fishing and birding.

THE GOYT VALLEY

MAP REF SK0175

The River Goyt meets the River Tame in Stockport to form the famous River Mersey. Its upper and middle reaches cleave a deep, gorge-like valley through some of the most accessible moorland in the Peak District. This is an area that is threaded with by-roads, packhorse trails, and old railway tracks, a place where Cheshire meets Derbyshire amid a blaze of heather and bilberry-strewn uplands.

The Goyt River flows from south to north; it rises on the slopes of Cat and Fiddle Moor, a wild and windswept place with a reputation for having the worst weather. The moor is named after the Cat and Fiddle Inn, at 1,690ft (515m) it is the second-highest pub in England. Like other high-altitude hostelries, such as The Snake or Tan Hill, it was built in the turnpike era at the start of the 19th century and is still a welcome sight for traffic on the sinuous A537. There are few other buildings to be seen for miles around, but some facilities are available at Derbyshire Bridge, which is the usual starting point to explore the Goyt Valley.

Years ago the Goyt was as natural an upland valley as is possible in England, but the original scatter of ancient oaks has now been augmented or replaced by conifer plantations and the river and meadowlands were flooded to create the Fernilee and Errwood reservoirs. The combination of lake and forest, cobalt and viridian beneath the magenta of heather moorland, rising to the highest point in Cheshire at nearby Shining Tor, 1,834 feet (559m), makes the Goyt a colourful place; parking and picnic sites around the reservoir shores and the walks through the woodlands draw so many walkers and visitors that there is a one-way system up the narrow road to Derbyshire Bridge – on summer Sundays and Bank Holidays this road is closed to traffic.

Insight

PEAK PANTHER

On a bright winter's day in 1995 a small group of birdwatchers saw something out of the ordinary. While wandering by the hedge along the western shores of Combs Reservoir they came across some large clawed footprints measuring 3.5in (89mm) wide, which were sunk deep into the mud. The prints didn't belong to a dog. After studying the photographs they had taken, it became obvious that a huge cat had been on the prowl – probably the infamous Peak Panther that has had may sightings in the hills above Chinley and Hayfield.

Visit

GOYT'S MOSS

Below Cat and Fiddle Moor is Goyt's Moss, a colourful carpet of cotton grass and asphodel belying a treacherous surface of wet peat. In late April and May golden plovers and curlews add their voices to those of pipits and larks; this is also the breeding ground of the twite, a small finch with a pink rump.

FERNILEE RESERVOIR

A Buxton Figure of Eight

An attraction in its own right, Buxton lies at the heart of outstanding countryside, and high roads with magnificent views that radiate from it. This tour makes the most of the town's situation with a figure-of-eight route, out on the shoulder of the Goyt, back via Chapel-en-le-Frith and Dove Holes, then out again on the dramatic Axe Edge road and down towards Leek, before returning through quiet rolling farmland.

Route Directions

1 From Buxton, just above the Opera House, take the A5004 uphill towards Whaley Bridge, rising for a mile (1.6km) through woodland and then over moorland. After another half mile (800m) a cairn on the right marks the National Park boundary. Continue for 2.5 miles (4km) along the shoulder of the valley to the Upper Hall lay-by (wonderful views). Drive on for another 2 miles (3.2km), through Fernilee to the outskirts of Whaley Bridge, where you turn right along the B5470, signed 'Chapel-en-le-Frith'. Pass by The Board pub and on for another 3 miles (4.8km) through Tunstead Milton to enter Chapel-en-le-Frith. Turn off at the Kings Arms, on the left, if you want to explore the centre of this old town.

2 Drive along the B5470 through Chapel-en-le-Frith for another mile (1.6km), past the Old Packhorse Inn on the left, then turn left following the sign for the A6 and Buxton. Go under the flyover and then turn right to join the A6, along a wooded valley for 2 miles (3.2km) to Dove Holes. The workaday quarry village hides the site of a prehistoric henge. Despite the noise from the quarries and traffic from the A6, you'll doubtless find the remains impressive.

3 Continue on the A6 for 3 miles (4.8km) to Fairfield, a pretty village on the outskirts of Buxton. The road descends into the middle of Buxton; at the bottom, follow the signs for the A53 to Leek, via four roundabouts but well signed, with the dome of the former Devonshire Hospital to your right. Begin the second loop of the tour by following the A53 towards Leek, passing the Pavilion Gardens on your left. Continue uphill out of town for 2 miles (3.2km), through traffic lights and out on to open hilltops – the start of Axe Edge. The Dove and Manifold rivers rise here. The road gradually descends past a side road to Flash and out of Derbyshire into Staffordshire, then continues on for about 3 miles (4.8km) to Ramshaw Rocks on the right. Ramshaw Rocks include a feature which looks like a face The Winking Man appears to wink at you if you drive north.

4 Continue on the A53 for another 1.5 miles (2.4km), down to Upper Hulme and Blackshaw Moor and off the high moorland. In 2 miles (3.2km) pass the Moss Rose Inn on the outskirts of Leek, then in less than half a mile (800m) turn left onto Springfield Road, signed for Ashbourne and Derby. Shortly reach a junction with the A523; turn right to visit Leek or left to continue the tour. Leek is a thriving market town and antiques centre.

5 Head uphill through rolling pastureland for 2.5 miles (4km) and pass a turn to the RSPB Nature Reserve of Combes Valley, then on for 1.5 miles (2.4km) to Bottom House crossroads and the Green Man Inn. Turn left along the B5053 signed for Longnor and continue for 1.5 miles (2.4km) through Onecote. After 2.5 miles (4km) the road twists down to cross the pretty Warslow Brook, a tributary of the Manifold, then rises for a mile (1.6km) to the village of Warslow. Continue along the B5053 for 4 miles (6.4km), crossing the River Manifold before climbing sharply into Longnor. Longnor is a compact and attractive village amidst farming country.

6 Go ahead left up out of the village (between the stores and The Horseshoe pub), cresting a ridge in 0.5 mile (800m) – beware of the traffic lights – before crossing the River Dove at Glutton Bridge, back into Derbyshire. The landscape changes quite abruptly as the road follows a limestone gorge (Glutton Dale) for half a mile (800m) up to a crossroads (Dalehead to the left, Earl Sterndale to the right). Keep ahead here; the road shortly curves to the left across a steep slope and rises to a crest before dropping past the quarries at Hind Low to a T-junction at Brierlow Bar. Turn left along the A515 and drive for 3 miles (4.8km) to return to Buxton town centre and the start point of the drive.

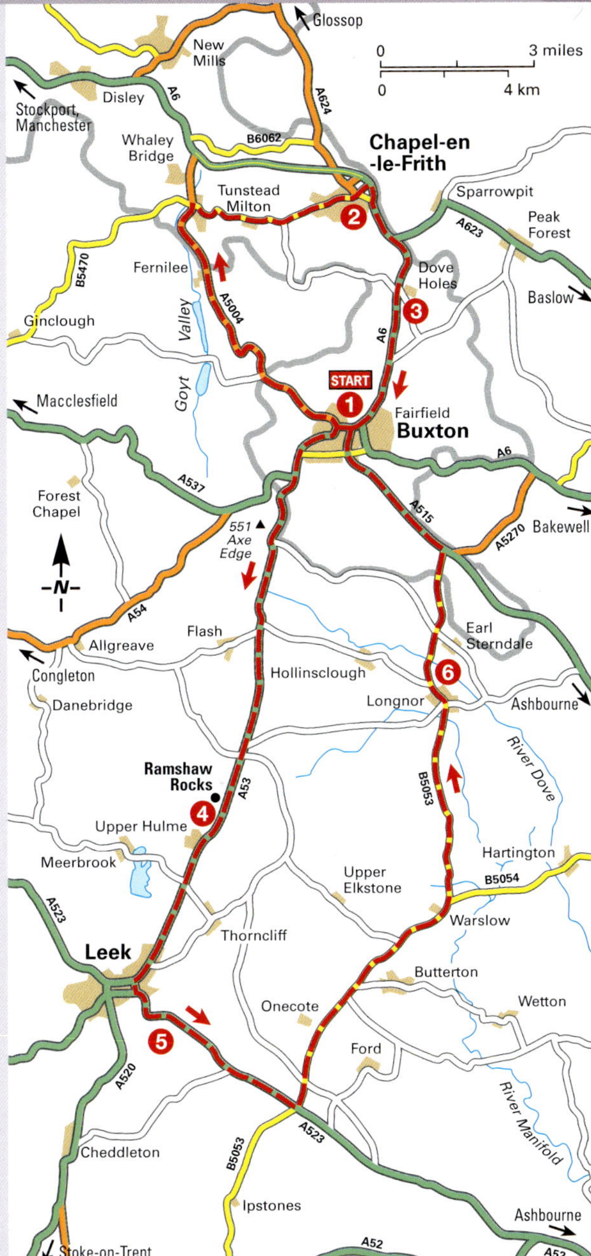

Macclesfield Forest

This circular walk explores the old and new Macclesfield Forest, and the mini Matterhorn of Shutlingsloe. Looming above Wildboarclough is the coned peak of Shutlingsloe, which at 1,659ft (506m) offers a full 360-degree panoramic view over Cheshire, Staffordshire and Derbyshire. Especially prominent is Tegg's Nose, a gritstone outcrop to the north that protrudes above the dark green conifers of the present-day Macclesfield Forest.

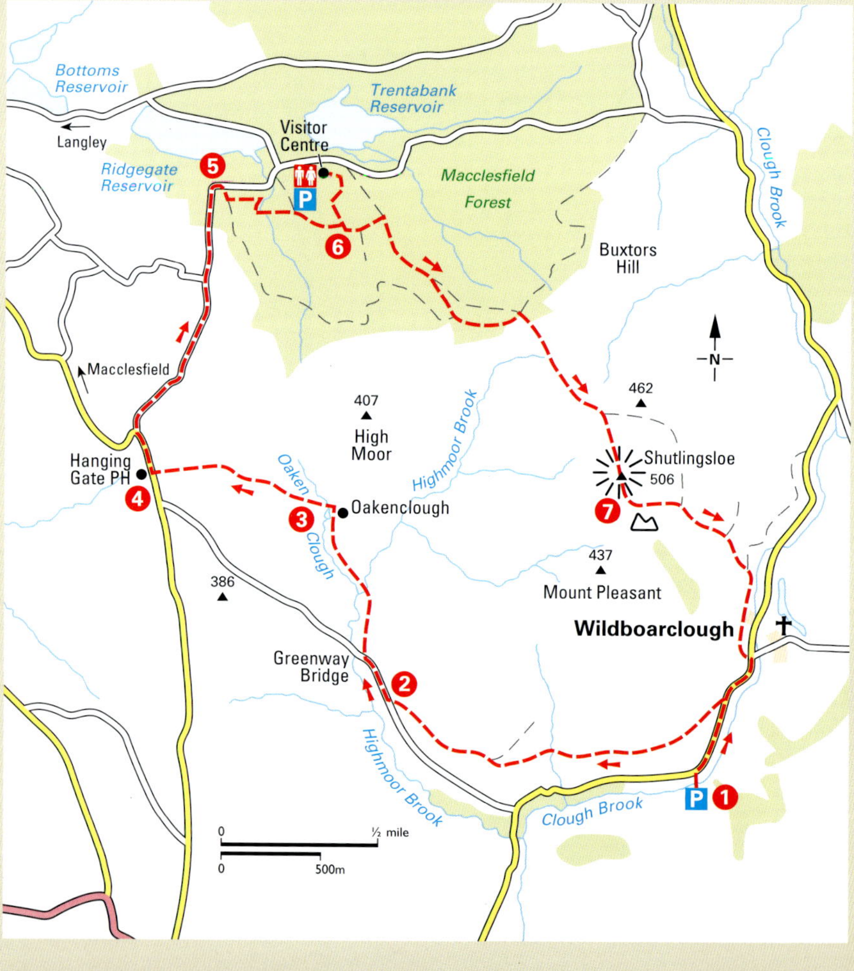

Route Directions

1 Walk along the road for 440yds (402m) to a private house, then at the foot of its drive go over a stile on the left for a path across a sloping field. This maintains its direction through successive fields (each with a wall gate) until finally you reach the tarmac farm drive at the very top. Turn left and walk along this drive to the lane.

2 Turn right at the far end and walk along the lane as far as Greenway Bridge. Go over a stile on the right and follow the path beside the stream, until it crosses it in order to veer left, up Oakenclough. Keep to the bottom of this little valley, past a ruined stone shelter, and as it rises continue to its far head, near a small pond. Turn right on to a private drive and then go almost immediately left for a wall-side path uphill.

3 At the top go over a stile and strike out across moorland on a clear grassy track. Maintain your direction until you reach a stile on the far side. Go over this and then descend on a sunken, fenced track to emerge opposite the Hanging Gate pub.

4 Turn right and follow the road for a mile (1.6km), keeping straight on at the junction where the road bends sharply left. Ignore another turning on the left, until finally the lane turns right, into Macclesfield Forest, where there's a wide gate on the right.

5 Don't go through the main gate. Instead go over the stile to the left, signposted 'Shutlingsloe/Trentabank', and follow the footpath which runs parallel with the lane. After dropping down to a newly planted area, cross the footbridge and at the junction of tracks near the wood sculpture carry straight on up a wide, stony route. At the far end turn right, or for the visitor centre and toilets at Trentabank turn left.

6 Walk up the wide forest drive and go left at a fork, then at the far end turn right for a long but quite easy gravel track up through the trees. At the top go through a gate and continue straight on, then turn right to leave the forest for a stone-flagged path across the open moorland up towards the distinctive top of Shutlingsloe.

7 From the summit descend the eroded track down the steep eastern slope of the hill, until you eventually turn right on to an open farm drive. Follow this all the way down to the road and turn right to the car park.

Route facts

DISTANCE/TIME 7 miles (11.3km) 3hrs 30min

MAP OS Explorer OL24 White Peak

START Grid reference: SJ 98068

TRACKS Sloping field paths, lanes and easy forest tracks, steep hillside, lots of stiles. Rough pasture, angular hills, plus large tracts of woodland

GETTING TO THE START Take the A537 from Macclesfield towards Buxton. Turn sharp right to take the A54. Follow signs to Macclesfield Forest. Parking is at a lay-by at Brookside on a lane 0.75 miles (1.2km) south of Wildboarclough.

THE PUB The Hanging Gate, Higher Sutton. Tel: 01260 227239

❶ This is a challenging walk.

LEEK MAP REF SJ9856

The little Staffordshire mill town of Leek sits on a broad low hill in a bend of the River Churnet. Unlike most of the other towns circling the Peak District, Leek is not overshadowed by the hills and makes no extravagant claims to be an adventure centre. All around are green valleys and rolling pastures, full of dairy cattle and longwool sheep. To the south lies the Churnet, with a host of visitor attractions, such as the Caldon Canal, the Cheddleton Railway Centre and the old Cheddleton Flint Mill. To the southwest is Stoke-on-Trent with its fine pottery heritage. But to the north and east the foothills rise inexorably to heather moorland and limestone plateaux; like Macclesfield and Glossop there is a sense of a settlement butting as closely to the hills as it dared, exploiting the power of the elements.

Textiles transformed Leek from an old medieval market town to an industrial centre, but silk was the speciality, which meant that many of the early mills were small and clean, with better working conditions than those endured in the cotton mills of the Peak valleys. Most of the mill buildings are now put to other uses, but the wealth generated by silk is recalled in the many imposing buildings commissioned from the Victorian architects William and Larner Sugden.

The heart of old Leek, easily missed on a fleeting visit, is the cobbled-stone Market Place. At one end of it stands the 17th-century Butter Cross, a link with the town's dairying tradition. The cross was removed from its original location, at the lower side of the square towards Sheep Market, nearly 200 years ago and has since been restored. An attractive watermill stands at the edge of the town as a monument to James Brindley, the 18th-century canal engineer.

Further upstream, a tributary of the Churnet was dammed to create Rudyard Lake, to supply water for his Trent and Mersey Canal.

A few miles north of the town, the Churnet itself has been dammed to form Tittesworth Reservoir, with facilities including a visitor centre, woodland walks, car parks and a bird hide overlooking the shallow northern corner.

Insight

'SCHEMER' BRINDLEY

James Brindley, Leek's most famous son, was actually born at Wormhill, near Tideswell, but his family moved to Leek in 1726 when he was ten years old. He was apprenticed to a millwright at Sutton, near Macclesfield, when he was 17 and was soon solving all sorts of engineering problems. Most of his ideas worked, and he was nicknamed 'Schemer'. Wealth and notoriety followed, but in his later years he became famous for his canal designs, particularly the Trent and Mersey and its Harecastle Tunnel. Brindley died from pneumonia in 1772.

LYME PARK MAP REF SJ9682

Lyme Park (National Trust) on the western edge of the Peak District is a modest mirror image of Chatsworth. The imposing Hall is a leading example of the Palladian style, the work of the Italian architect Giacomo Leoni in the 1720's; it featured as 'Pemberley' in the 1995 BBC adaptation of *Pride and Prejudice*. The interior, a heady mix of Elizabethan and later rooms, houses remarkable Mortlake tapestries and the Lyme Caxton Missal prayer-book.

Lyme was the home of the Legh family for 600 years and has sufficient style to make it one of the top visitor attractions in the area, set in a rural idyll of gardens, parkland and moorland, yet only a stone's throw from Stockport.

Those who prefer outdoor attractions to the splendours of the stately home will enjoy the wildfowl on the lake and herds of red and fallow deer among the trees. The 1,300-acre (520ha) park also has excellent short walks and viewpoints: a modest alternative to the high hills if the weather is closing in.

MACCLESFIELD

MAP REF SJ9173

The town of Macclesfield sits firmly at the foot of the hills, close enough to suffer draughts of frost-laden air and share any low cloud. Specialising in silk was its salvation but also its downfall. From a market town, Macclesfield first became known for buttons, then for all kinds of silken products. By the mid-19th century the town was bursting at the seams, with 56 silk 'throwsters' (producing the thread or thrown silk) and 86 businesses creating silk fabric or finished goods. Despite this success, or perhaps because of it, the workforce lived in wretched conditions, with an appalling level of infant mortality, and with nowhere to go when the industry hit one of its frequent declines.

Silk mills, chapels and banks – solid square buildings of blackened stone – are scattered through the town today. Among them is the huge Sunday School on Roe Street, which is now a heritage centre with a silk museum and shop. Near the old market cross, behind St Michael's Church and its beautiful soot-covered chapel of 1501, lies a narrow garden terrace known as Sparrow Park (officially, the Broadhurst Memorial Gardens). This is a pivot of the old town, a place to stop and ponder its rich and chequered history. Below the gardens there is a steep bank, down which run the picturesque 108 Steps. There is a view through the shrubs of the railway station and over the hinterland of the town, to green remembered foothills at the western face of the Peak.

On the farmland of the foothills, above Sutton Lane Ends and a growing patchwork of housing estates, lie the two Langley reservoirs. They were built in the mid-19th century to provide clean water for Macclesfield, as a response to infant mortality and disease among the mill workers. But young Charles Tunnicliffe, the famous country artist, knew them in more peaceful times as a haunt of sandpiper and moorhens. Further into the hills are Ridgegate and Trentabank reservoirs, the winter resort of pochard and goldeneye; Cheshire's largest heronry is also here. Then comes the conifer blanket of Macclesfield Forest, once part of a vast royal hunting forest.

Close to Trentabank is a Forest Visitor Centre, from where there are walks and drives. At the eastern edge of the forest lies the tiny Chapel of St Stephen, where a rush-bearing ceremony takes place each August. At the highest southern access point there is a path that leads onto open moorland and up to Shutlingsloe, a distinctive Peak summit.

About 3 miles (4.8km) south of Macclesfield is Gawsworth Hall, a fine Tudor black-and-white manor house, which was the birthplace of Mary Fitton. This renowned lady is thought by some to be the 'Dark Lady' of Shakespeare's sonnets, who aroused such emotional turmoil in the poet. We shall probably never know, but the house is worth a visit anyway, for its wonderful old timberwork, its paintings and its suits of armour. The grounds, thought to be a rare example of an Elizabethan pleasure garden, include a tilting ground and are the venue for open-air theatre and craft fairs during the summer months.

THE ROACHES

MAP REF SK0062

There are few real peaks in the Peak District (the name is derived from the Old English *pecsaetan*, meaning hill-dwellers), but the most elegant and craggy-topped are in the far west: Hen Cloud, Ramshaw Rocks and The Roaches. They are gritstone outcrops, similar to those in the Dark Peak and Eastern Moors, but here they were more heavily contorted or squashed together, leading to a landscape of misfit valleys, steep slopes and rock faces rather than plateau moorland.

Ramshaw Rocks are probably the best-known outlier of the Roaches, because they tower above the roadside on the A53 north of Leek and have a face-like formation. The A53 and the quiet winding roads to the west of Axe Edge lead to some interesting places.

Axe Edge itself is too high to be anything but wild. One notable village tucked away just off the main road is Flash, claimed to be the highest village in England at 1,518 feet (462m). The River Dane rises nearby, jinking a course between hills and ridges and flowing southwest to Gradbach and Danebridge: this is delightful countryside full of trees and meadows, barns and cowslip banks.

The Roaches ridge lies a few miles to the southwest of Flash and runs northwest to southeast, its main rock-climbing exposures facing the setting sun. A footpath follows the crest of the ridge, linking with Back Forest and creating a 4-mile (6.4km) ridge walk with superb views. Heather clothes the upper hills, bracken and woodland the slopes. The area has become famous as the home of a colony of red-necked wallabies, a Tasmanian oddity that arrived at a private zoo at Swythamley Hall in the 1930s and escaped to form a wild population; some were photographed here in 2009.

WHALEY BRIDGE

MAP REF SK0081

This little town grew up with dust on its face and Goyt water in its veins. Coal and textiles provided the only gainful work – both have now gone. These days there is hardly a whisper of past industry and employment is more varied. Visitors call in on their way to the Goyt Valley or to visit the Peak Forest Canal. The basin in the town is engaging, but the true glory of the waterway is at Buxworth, 0.5 miles (800m) to the east, where an extraordinary canal and tramroad interchange has been restored. The canal was built to convey limestone from nearby upland quarries to Manchester; at Buxworth the rock was processed and put into narrowboats

South of the town is Toddbrook Reservoir, built to feed the Peak Forest Canal, and tiny Taxal village clustered around its church. Inside St James's are memorials to the Jodrell family, and a monument to Michael Heathcote, 'Gentleman of the Pantry and Yeoman of the Mouth to His Late Majesty King George the Second'. Heathcote lived to be 75 years old, so presumably nobody tried to poison the king during his time as official food-taster.

WILDBOARCLOUGH

MAP REF SJ9868

Only a few outbuildings remain of the Crag Mills that once made this valley have the hum of a minor industrial centre, which employed more than 600 people. The mills here specialised in bleaching, printing and dyeing of first cotton, then later carpets.

Along the valley today you'll find that most traces of the village's industrial heritage are camouflaged green. There are shrub-covered foundations, grassy trackways and mossy walls. The stream boasts pretty waterfalls and deep pools and is the territory of dippers and grey wagtails. The impression is of a rural backwater, at the foot of Shutlingsloe, the 'Cheshire Matterhorn'.

Activity

TEGG'S NOSE AND THE GRITSTONE TRAIL

The best introduction to the Cheshire slice of the Peak landscape is from Tegg's Nose Country Park, along Buxton Old Road to the east of Macclesfield. There are superb views from the Windy Way car park and walks along a network of tracks and pathways, by the old quarry or down through woodland to the reservoirs above Langley. It is possible at this point to join the Gritstone Trail, a waymarked footpath running the length of Cheshire from Lyme Park to Mow Cop.

Insight

BEYOND THE LAW

Below Cut-thorn Hill lies Three Shires Head, where a packhorse bridge stands at the cusp between Derbyshire, Cheshire and Staffordshire. Many years ago, this was where illegal prizefights took place because the local police forces had no authority to pursue suspects beyond their own county boundary. For the very same reason, Flash became the capital of coin counterfeiting, and the word Flash ('Flash Harry', 'flash money' etc) entered the language to denote a fake.

Insight

WILD COUNTRY

It is difficult to imagine this sweep of country as a dangerous, lonely wilderness, but names on the map like Wolf End and Wildboarclough hint at the reputation that it once enjoyed. This is one of several locations claimed as the place where the last wild boar in England was killed (although nowadays they again forage in the woodlands of Kent, East Sussex and Gloucestershire).

Flash Village

Look for evidence of the network of packhorse trails on the moors covered by this walk. These ancient routes were used from medieval times to transport goods between communities. Today you will find these paved routes across the moors, descending into the valleys in distinctive 'hollow ways' or sunken lanes.

Route Directions

1 Walk through the village, pass the New Inn and an old chapel. Turn right at a footpath sign and head towards the last house. Go over a stile, turn right and follow the path over two walls. Veer left towards a gate in the corner of the field to a

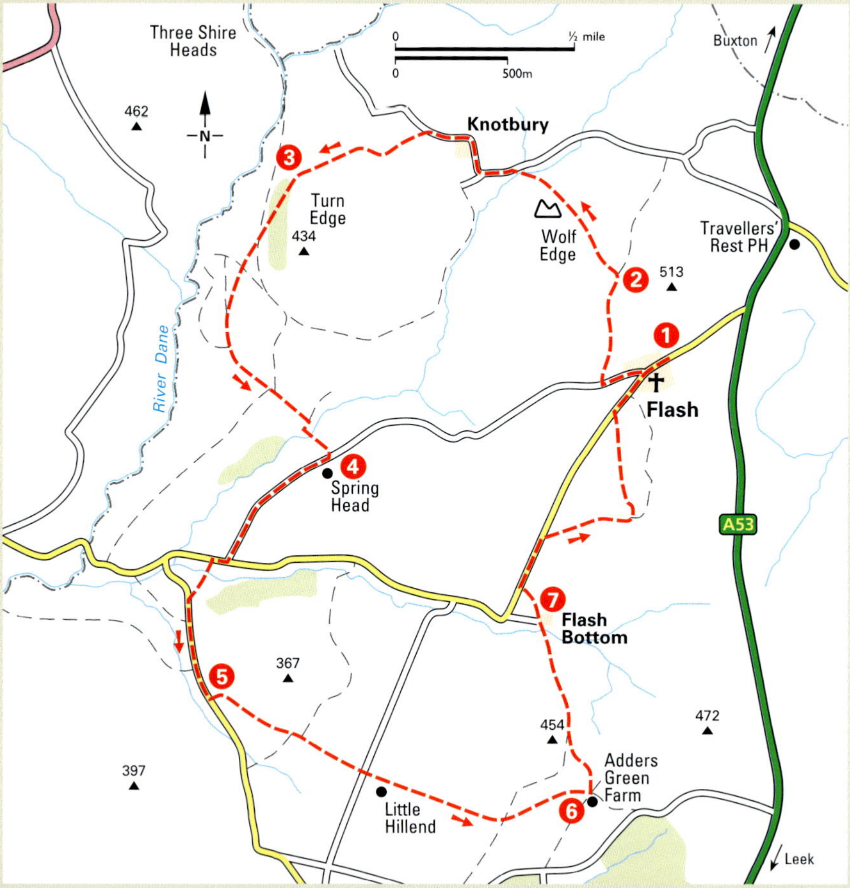

lane between walls. Cross another stile then turn left at a waymarker.

2 Continue through a gate then follow the waymarker right and uphill to Wolf Edge. Pass the rocks, veer left downhill over a stile and across heather moorland. Cross a stile on the right and continue downhill to a marker post. Cross the wall, then a bridge and turn left on to the road. Go right at the junction and follow this road through Knotbury then, after the last house on the left, take the path on the left, crossing several stiles over the moorland.

3 Follow this path downhill, go left along a farm track, then resume the downward route through fields and join another track. Veer right of the road at the next waymarker, cross a stile then keep straight ahead at the next signpost. Follow this track until it crosses a bridge, then heads uphill.

4 Opposite Spring Head turn right on to the road. At the junction, turn right then left through a gap stile. Go downhill, over a bridge, then uphill following the path, left across the field, through a gap stile and turn left on the road.

5 Go left at the next signpost, following the waymarked path to a farm track. At some farm buildings go through a gate and then fork right. Continue to the road, cross it then continue on the path through Little Hillend. Follow this waymarked path to Adders Green Farm.

6 Turn left, through a gate and along a wall. At the end of the wall turn left, follow the wall, cross a gate and then follow the path round the foot of the hill and through a gate to Flash Bottom. Go through a small gate, turn left and up to the driveway.

7 Go through a gate opposite, follow the path over a field and up steps to the road. Turn right, then right again at the next sign. Cross several fields on a well waymarked path towards farm buildings. Cross over a stream then head uphill to the left to rejoin the road back to Flash.

Route facts

DISTANCE/TIME 6 miles (9.7km) 4h

MAP OS Explorer OL24 White Peak

START Flash village; parking on roadside near school, grid ref SK 026672

TRACKS Some on road but mostly footpaths that can be boggy in wet weather. Around 35 stiles and gates

GETTING TO THE START
Flash village is off the A53 between Buxton and Leek. Drive south from Buxton for just over 4 miles (6.4km) passing The Travellers' Rest pub on your left. In a further 0.25 miles (400m), fork right onto a minor road to Flash. Park taking care on the roadside before the school.

THE PUB Travellers' Rest, Flash. Tel: 01298 23695

❗ The route explores a relatively remote area of and should not be attempted in bad weather, especially in low cloud or mist. Suitable for adventurous older children/family groups.

Combs Reservoir

Combs lies beneath the sombre crag-fringed slopes of Combs Moss. This route starts by the west side of the dam on a narrow path between the lake and Meveril Brook. Beyond the reservoir the path tucks under the railway, leads into Combs village then heads for the hillsides before returning to the shores of the reservoir.

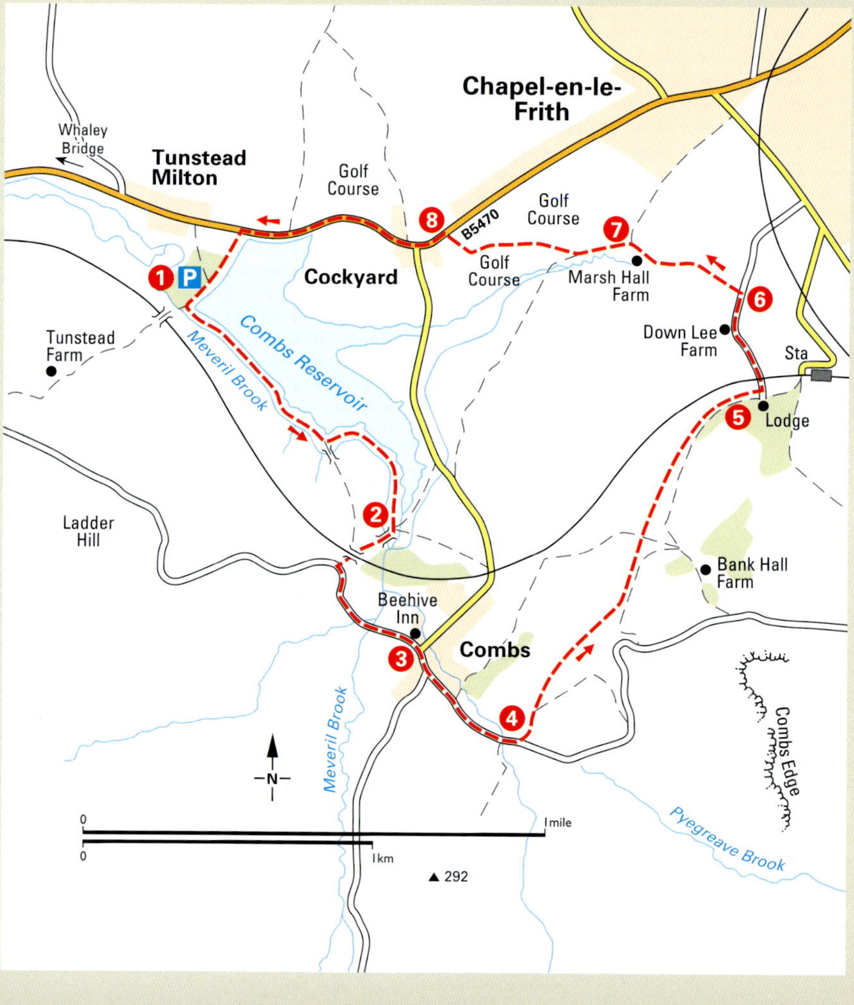

Route Directions

1 Follow the path leading from the dam along the reservoir's western shore, ignoring the first footbridge over Meveril Brook.

2 As the reservoir narrows the path traverses small fields, then comes to another footbridge over the brook. This time cross it and head south across another field. Beyond a foot tunnel under the Buxton line railway, the path reaches a narrow hedge-lined country lane. Turn left along the lane into Combs village.

3 Past the Beehive Inn in the village centre, take the lane straight ahead, then the left fork, signposted to Dove Holes. This climbs out of the village towards Combs Edge.

4 Take the second footpath on the left, which begins at a muddy clearing just beyond Millway Cottage. Go through the stile and climb on a partially slabbed path and then uphill across pasture with the wall on your right. Away to the right is the huge comb of Pygreave Brook. Climb the pathless spur and go through gateways in the next two boundary walls before following a wall on the right. Ignore a gate in this wall – that's a path to Bank Hall Farm – but stay with the narrow path raking across rough grassy hillslopes with the railway line and the reservoir below left.

5 The path comes down to a track that runs alongside the railway line. This joins a lane just short of the Lodge. Turn left to go under the railway and north to Down Lee Farm.

6 Turn left through a kissing gate 200yds (183m) beyond the farmhouse. The signposted path follows an overgrown hedge towards Marsh Hall Farm. The fields can become very boggy on the final approaches. When you reach the farm complex turn right over a stile and then follow a vehicle track heading northwest.

7 After 200yds (183m) turn left on a field path that heads west to a stile at the edge of the Chapel-en-le-Frith golf course. Waymarking arrows show the way across the fairway. The stile marking the exit from the golf course is 300yds (274m) short of the clubhouse. You then cross a small field to reach the B5470.

Route facts

DISTANCE/TIME 3 miles (4.8km) 2h30

MAP Explorer OL24 White Peak

START Combs Reservoir car park, grid ref SK 033797

TRACKS Can be muddy, several stiles

GETTING TO THE START
The car park at Combs Reservoir is in the village of Tunstead Milton, about 2 miles (3.2km) southeast of Whaley Bridge on the B5470 towards Chapel-en-le-Frith. Look on the right for a no-through road sign, a small lodge and a British Waterways board for the reservoir; the car park is at the western end of the dam.

THE PUB The Beehive Inn, Combs. Tel: 01298 812758; www.thebeehiveinn.co.uk

8 Turn left along the road (there's a pavement on the far side), and follow it past the Hanging Gate pub at Cockyard. After passing the entrance to the sailing club, turn left to cross over the dam of Combs Reservoir and return to the car park.

TOURIST INFORMATION CENTRES

Buxton
The Pavilion.
Tel: 01298 25106;
www.visitbuxton.co.uk

Leek
Market Place.
Tel: 01538 483741;
www.discoverstaffordshire peakdistrict.com

Macclesfield
Council Offices, Town Hall.
Tel: 01625 504114;
www.peaksandplains.co.uk

PLACES OF INTEREST

Brindley Mill
Mill Street, Leek.
Tel: 01538 483741;
www.brindleymill.net

Buxton Museum and Art Gallery
Peak Buildings, Terrace Road. Tel: 01298 24658

Cheddleton Flint Mill
Leek Road, Cheddleton.
Tel: 0161 408 5083. Free.

Chestnut Centre
Castleton Road, Chapel-en-le-Frith. Tel: 01298 814099;
www.ottersandowls.co.uk
Otter haven, owl sanctuary.

Churnet Valley Railway
Cheddleton Station,
Churnet Valley Railway.
Tel: 01538 360522; www.churnet-valley-railway.co.uk

Dunge Valley Hidden Gardens
Windgather, Kettleshulme.
Tel: 01663 733787;
www.dungevalley.co.uk

Hare Hill
4 miles (6.4km) north of Macclesfield off B5087.
Tel: 01625 584412

Lyme Park
Disley. Tel: 01663 762023;
www.nationaltrust.org.uk

Macclesfield Silk Heritage
Heritage Centre, Roe Street.
Tel: 01625 613210

Pavilion Gardens
Buxton. Tel: 01298 23114
Free.

Poole's Cavern
Green Lane, Buxton.
Tel: 01298 26978;
www.poolescavern.co.uk

Silk Museum & Paradise Mill
Park Lane, Macclesfield.
Tel: 01625 612045; www.macclesfield.silk.museum

West Park Museum
Prestbury Road, Macclesfield.
Tel: 01625 619831

FOR CHILDREN

Blackbrook Zoological Park
Winkhill, nr Leek.
Tel: 01538 308293;
www.blackbrookzoo.co.uk

Blaze Farm
Wildboarclough.
Tel: 01260 227229;
www.blazefarm.com

Freshfields Donkey Village
Wormhill Road, Peak Forest.
Tel: 01298 79775;
www.donkey-village.org.uk
Donation requested.

Rudyard Lake Steam Railway
Tel: 01995 672280;
www.rlst.org.uk

SHOPPING

Buxton
Market, Tue and Sat.

Chapel-en-le-Frith
Market, Thu.

Leek
Market, Wed and Sat.

Macclesfield
Outdoor market, Tue, Fri, Sat.

LOCAL SPECIALITIES

Farmers Markets
Buxton, first Thu.
Leek, 3rd Sat each month.
Macclesfield, 3rd Fri each month.
Whaley Bridge, 2nd Sat each month.

Spa Water
Spa water from the fountain in The Crescent, Buxton.

PERFORMING ARTS

Buxton
Opera House, Water Street, Buxton. Tel: 01298 72190;
www.buxton-opera.co.uk

SPORTS & ACTIVITIES

ANGLING

Fly Fishing
Danebridge Fisheries, Wincle.
Tel: 01260 227293
Errwood Reservoir, Goyt Valley. Tel: 01663 734220
Lamaload Reservoir, Macclesfield.
Tel: 01625 619935

Coarse
Combs Reservoir, Whaley Bridge. Tel: 01663 762393
Rudyard Lake.
Tel: 01538 306280;
www.rudyardlake.com

BOAT HIRE/SAILING
Rudyard Lake
Tel: 01538 306280
Tittesworth Reservoir
Tel: 01782 722226;
www.peakpursuits.co.uk
COUNTRY PARKS AND NATURE RESERVES
Grinlow and Buxton Country Park.
Tegg's Nose Country Park, Macclesfield.
Tel: 01625 614278
Tittesworth Reservoir.
Tel: 01538 300400
CYCLING
Macclesfield Forest
On and off-road routes.
Rudyard Lake, near Leek
Level cycling trail on old railway beside Rudyard Lake.
The Middlewood Way
Runs northwards from Macclesfield to Marple.
CYCLE HIRE
Parsley Hay
Parsley Hay Bike Hire.
Tel: 01298 84493
GUIDED WALKS
Professional Blue Badge Guides. Tel: 01629 534284
Buxton
From Tourist Information Centre. Tel: 01298 25106
Etherow–Goyt Walks
Etherow Country Park.
Tel: 01614 276937
Leek
Town walks from Leek Tourist Information Centre.
Tel: 01538 483741
Peak District
Annual Peak District Walking Festival. Guided walks.
Tel: 0870 444 7275; www.visitpeakdistrict.com/walk
Walking the Bollin Valley
Tel: 01625 534790
National Park Walks with a Ranger
Peak District National Park.
Tel: 01629 816200;
www.peakdistrict.gov.uk
HANG-GLIDING
Leek
Peak Hang Gliding Centre, 8 Whitfield Street, Leek.
Tel: 07000 426465;
www.peakhanggliding.co.uk
HORSE-RIDING
Buxton
Buxton Riding Centre, Fern Farm. Tel: 01298 72319;
www.fernfarmcottages.co.uk
Flash
Northfield Farm Riding & Trekking Centre, Flash.
Tel: 01298 22543;
www.northfieldfarm.co.uk
LONG-DISTANCE FOOTPATHS & TRAILS
The Gritstone Trail
35 miles (56km) from Disley in Cheshire to Kidsgrove in Staffordshire.
The Middlewood Way
11-mile (18km) trail between Macclesfield and Marple.
The Midshires Way
230 miles (370km) from Stockport to Buckinghamshire.
The Pennine Bridleway
350 miles (563km) from Cromford to Byrness (Northumberland).

ANNUAL EVENTS & CUSTOMS

For the full programme visit www.visitpeakdistrict.com
Well dressing in Chapel-en-le-Frith, Buxworth, Peak Forest and Buxton, Jul.
Buxton
Antiques Fair, May.
Brass Band Festival, May.
Buxton Festival, Jul.
Buxton Fringe Festival, Jul.
International Gilbert & Sullivan Festival, Jul/Aug.
Country Music Festival, Sep.
Cheddleton
Carnival, Aug.
Flash
Teapot Parade, Jun.
Well-dressing, mid-Jun.
Leek
Leek Arts Festival and Carnival, May.
Leek & District Show, Jul.
Macclesfield
Sheep Dog Trials, Aug.
Macclesfield Forest
Rush-bearing ceremony, St Stephen's Church, Aug.

THE ROACHES

Tea Rooms

Brookside Café

Wildboarclough, Macclesfield, Cheshire SK11 0BD. Tel: 01260 227632

Popular with ramblers and cyclists in this corner of the Peak District, the Brookside has been offering sustenance for more than 40 years. Expect great home-cooking, from afternoon teas to wholesome meals, served amid stunning countryside.

The Coffee Shop

Lyme Park, Disley, Cheshire SK12 2NX. Tel: 01663 762023

In the shadow of Lyme Hall, this unpretentious and welcoming place offers simple, filling fare. There's a more extensive restaurant in Lyme Hall itself.

Roaches Tea Rooms

Paddock Farm, Upper Hulme, Leek, Staffordshire, ST13 5SE. Tel: 01538 300345; www.roachestearooms.co.uk

A very homely place at which to indulge in that local delicacy, the Staffordshire oatcake (a dream with bacon and cheese), cream teas, calorific treats or maybe just a mug of tea, enjoying the remarkable scenery of The Roaches. The friendly folk at Paddock Farm cater for walkers and climbers.

The Coffee Tavern

Shrigley Road, Pott Shrigley, Bollington, Cheshire SK10 5SE Tel: 01625 576370

This is a firm favourite with walkers, cyclists and diners in these western fringes of the Peak District. Here you can enjoy anything from a modest pot of tea and a cake or a light snack to a three-course meal.

Pubs

The Swan Inn

Macclesfield Road, Kettleshulme, Whaley Bridge, Cheshire SK23 7QU Tel: 01663 732943

Once rescued from closure by a consortium of villagers, and now under new ownership this tiny pub is a champion of local beers, complementing the range of largely locally sourced food. It's the perfect place to unwind after a good walk.

The Ship Inn

Wincle, Cheshire SK11 0QE Tel: 01260 227217

This pub clings to the steep side of the Dane Valley above superb woodlands and the enticing ridges and clefts of the western Peak. Just two little rooms shelter happy drinkers of local beers and contented diners feasting on a superb menu strong on Cheshire produce.

Quiet Woman

Earl Sterndale, Buxton, Derbyshire SK17 9SL Tel: 01298 83211

There is no music here, just the hum of conversation over home-made pork pies washed down with Marstons and a couple of guest beers. Behind the pub is a smallholding with friendly stock to keep the kids entertained.

The Hanging Gate

Meg Lane, Higher Sutton, Macclesfield, Cheshire SK11 0NG. Tel: 01260 252238

Open fires, gnarled beams, country-cottage décor, exemplary food, beers from Hydes brewery; it's a mixture made in heaven, popular with ramblers and birdwatchers using Macclesfield Forest.

Navigation Inn

Brookside, Buxworth, High Peak, Derbyshire SK23 7NE Tel: 01663 732072; www.navigationinn.co.uk

Enjoy fine real ales from far and wide and tasty, traditional English cooking. Its comfy restaurant and the most time-honoured of bars make the Navigation Inn an unmissable destination.

ASHFORD IN THE WATER

White Peak

INTRODUCTION

Bakewell is the mid-point of the Peak District and through it runs the River Wye: downstream is the fine medieval mansion, Haddon Hall. Upstream the river quickens as the valley narrows surrounded by limestone hills. Little side valleys twist their way through the fossil seabed. Water often flows far below the ground, so that in past centuries village folk relied on wells, and gave thanks each summer for their constancy. The White Peak is a land of drystone walls and beautiful dales, of crouched churches and good pubs.

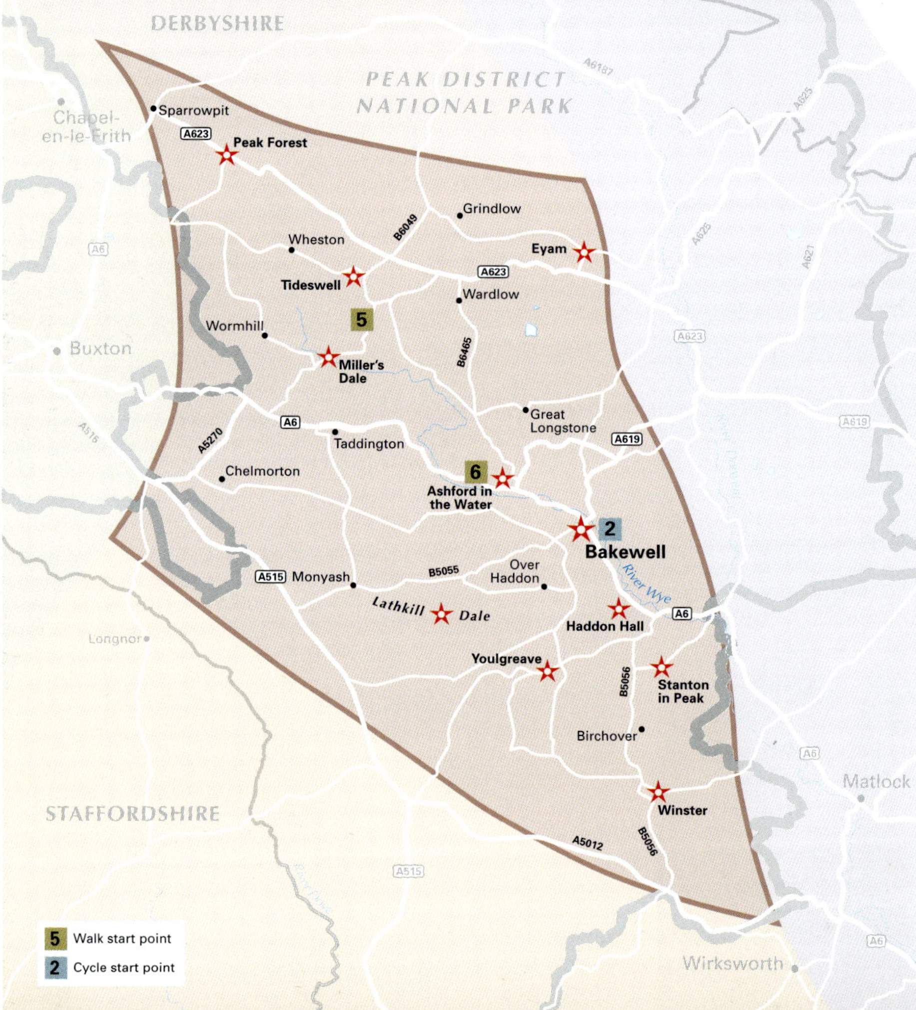

BAKEWELL

Unmissable attractions

The pale limestone plateau of the White Peak is criss-crossed by miles of drystone walls and dissected by steep-sided dales. It is a walkers' paradise with 1,600 miles (2,575km) of public footpaths crossing wild moor, along river banks or past sleepy villages. It is also crossed by the Tissington, High Peak and Monsal trails: former railway lines now converted to leisure routes for walkers and cyclists. Bakewell is the only town within the Peak District National Park and is celebrated for its famous pudding. Just downstream is the romantic medieval pile of Haddon Hall, frequently used as a film location. Two miles (3.2km) upstream is one of the most attractive of all the Peak villages, Ashford in the Water.

1

2

3

1 **Ashford in the Water**
Nestling on the banks of the River Wye, Ashford in the Water is one of the most attractive of the Peak villages. It is well known for its colourful Blessing of the Wells procession, which takes place annually on Trinity Sunday.

2 **Bakewell**
The original Bakewell Pudding was the result of a culinary misunderstanding between the local innkeeper and her cook. However, the recipe was such a success that a Mrs Wilson, wife of the local Tallow Chandler, started making the puddings for sale from this location in Bakewell from 1860 onwards.

3 **Monsal Dale**
A narrow footbridge spans the waters of the River Wye in Monsal Dale. Stop off at Monsal Head, above the valley (there is a large car park) to admire the far-reaching views of the dale and the river down below.

4 **Haddon Hall**
Dating from the 12th century, the splendid fortified medieval manor house of Haddon Hall has featured in many TV programmes and films including *Pride and Prejudice* (2005) starring Keira Knightly, Matthew MacFadyen and Dame Judi Dench.

5 **Tideswell**
Rows of stone-built terraced houses line the quaint alleyways and narrow lanes in Tideswell, one of the White Peak's many picturesque villages.

ASHFORD IN THE WATER

MAP REF SK1969

Only 2 miles (3.2km) from Bakewell and just off the busy A6, it is a wonder that Ashford in the Water has kept any kind of dignity. In fact it is one of the most attractive and interesting of all the Peak villages, sited on a twist of the River Wye, on the ancient port but bypassed by the new road.

Grassland and the A6 have taken the place of the 'black marble' quarry works on the approach to the village. 'Black marble' was an impure limestone that turned shiny black when polished; it was popular in Victorian times (for vases, fire-surrounds, etc.) and the works were extensive and probably represented the only blot on the Ashford horizon. This is not to say there had not been industry in the village before Henry Watson established his marble works in 1748. It simply means the scale was different. Many of the wonderful stone houses and cottages on the main triangle of lanes served as workshops when they were built; there was a corn mill, a candle-maker and several stocking mills. The community was more varied and the buildings more eccentric, and this has left a distinctive character to the place today, part pretty English village, part quirky Derbyshire jumble.

At the middle of Ashford is a green space, called Hall Orchard, once part of the grounds of Neville Hall, a medieval hunting lodge that stood on the eastern side. The space is now a playing field but there are some tall trees, notably limes, and around the rest of the village fine ash trees to offer shelter and shade. 'Oak won't grow in Ashford' goes the local saying, and this has proved true over the years.

On Church Street, between the Hall Orchard and the Wye, is a 17th-century tithe barn (now a private house) and the parish church. Most of the structure of the church is Victorian but just above the porch, returned to its original position, is a Norman tympanum. The Normans were not as expert as the Saxons at carving animals so there is some doubt about what the stone slab depicts. It may be a tree of life with a boar on one side and a lion on the other, or it may be meant to represent the Royal Forest with a boar and a wolf.

The main attraction for visitors to Ashford is the river, crystal clear and full of trout. There is space to wander along the banks, and three bridges, of which two are old. Close to the cricket field the bridge on the closed road carries an inscription 'M. Hyde 1664'; the brief memorial refers to The Reverend Hyde, who was thrown from his horse and drowned in the river below. Upstream, on an old packhorse trail, is the attractive

Visit

VIRGIN CROWNS

In Ashford church hang four 18th-century virgin crants, or crowns. These were funeral garlands, carried at maidens' funerals and then hung on beams or from the roof of the church. They are made of white paper attached to a wicker frame, and in the middle is a paper glove, bearing the name of the girl. The tradition of virgin crowns was widespread across England, but rarely do any of the fragile garlands survive to tell the sad tale.

Sheepwash Bridge; a stone fold on one side shows where the sheep were held before being plunged into the river and made to swim across to clean their fleeces.

Southwest of Ashford, on the dry-limestone plateau, is Sheldon, a small lead-mining village close to the famous Magpie Mine. The main shaft of the mine was 728 feet (222m) deep and water had to be pumped up to a sough, which carried it to the Wye on the curve below Great Shacklow Wood. In 1966 the roof of the sough collapsed and there was an explosion of pent-up mud and rocks. The resulting debris can still be seen today; the floodwater was gone all too quickly in a tidal wave.

Over the years Ashford has grown used to being flooded – 'in the Water' was added to the name quite recently.

BAKEWELL MAP REF SK2168

Bakewell is always busy with visitors and locals. Its streets are never free of traffic and bustle, but if you accept this from the outset there's every reason to enjoy the town; it is an exciting mixture of old and new, a tourist honeypot that is still thrives as a working community.

There are a surprisingly few very old buildings considering the rich history of Bakewell (it was granted a market and 15-day fair in 1254), but there are a number of fine 17th-century structures, such as the Market Hall, which serves as the Peak District National Park Information Centre, and the Town Hall. Up the steep road on the west side of the town stands an airy grass-covered knoll on which sits the lovely parish church of All Saints. Like many of the churches in Derbyshire it is broad and low, but with a spire as sharp as a 3H pencil. Inside you will find there are some fascinating fragments of Saxon and Norman stonework, and the famous

Insight

BAKEWELL PUDDINGS

The fame of the humble Bakewell Pudding has spread so far that it is now high on the list of favourite British puds. According to tradition, the recipe was the result of an error that emanated from the kitchen of the Rutland Arms Hotel in around 1860. The cook, flustered perhaps by a special order to prepare a strawberry tart for some very important guests, put the jam in first, then poured in the egg mixture designed for the pastry on top. Far from being a disaster, the new invention was hailed as a culinary triumph and became a regular item on the menu. Incidentally, don't ask for a Bakewell Tart in the home of their origin – they are always known here as 'puddings'. And please don't enquire who has the original recipe, included in the will of the cook at the Rutland Arms – it is still the cause of local dispute and rivalry!

Visit

TROUT WATCHING

One of the idlest pleasures on rivers like the Wye is to stand on a bridge and watch trout keeping stationary against the current below. Swimming against the flow looks remarkably easy, if you have the fins for it. Brown trout, with spotted flanks, are the native game fish made famous by *The Compleat Angler*; the rainbow trout is an American import, able to tolerate warmer and more polluted water.

Insight & Visit

GEOLOGY OF THE PLAGUE VILLAGE

Exploring the upper pathways of the village, such as the grassy alley from the Royal Oak up Little Edge and along May Walk, it is obvious that Eyam lies on the very edge of the limestone and only just qualifies as a White Peak village. In fact, most of the houses sited on the north side, towards Eyam Edge, were constructed using sandstone, which was the preferred building material, whilst the greyer, less durable limestone was used a few hundred yards away to the south. Just across the valley, and – perhaps understandably – rarely mentioned in tourist guidebooks, you can see two great working quarries, ripping into the hills for road-stone.

monument to Sir John Manners and his wife Dorothy, who are reputed to have eloped together from Haddon Hall in 1558. Outside the hall stands the shaft of a 9th-century stone cross, beautifully decorated with vine scrolls and figures. Nearby to the church is The Old House and Cunningham Place, a 16th-century parsonage now a museum.

Monday is market day in Bakewell, when cattle and sheep wagons converge behind Bridge Street and the market place is decked with awnings. Escaping the bleating and banter is very easy; the River Wye runs alongside, and within a few seconds it is possible to be out of the crowd and feeding ducks or trout along the river. Upstream is one of the oldest bridges in England, built in about 1300; impossible to appreciate if you are driving over it but a scene-stealer from water level where its five arches and solid breakwaters are visible. In the distance stands Castle Hill, where the settlement of Bakewell began in 920 with the establishment of a Mercian fort.

EYAM MAP REF SK2176

Disease was a fact of life in medieval England, and many of the Peak villages suffered the horrors of Black Death and plague. What made the weaving village of Eyam special was the attempt by the local rector, William Mompesson, to keep the outbreak in 1665–66 within the confines of the community and not let it be carried elsewhere. The whole village was put in quarantine, entire families tragically perished and Eyam became a byword for tragedy and self-sacrifice.

According to tradition, the plague virus was introduced into the village by a tailor called George Viccars, who bought some infected cloth from London. He died a few days after arriving at Eyam, lodging with Mary Cooper at what is now called Plague Cottage. A fortnight later Mary's son Edward died and the whole community braced itself for disaster. The young rector quickly sent his own children away, but stayed with his wife to care for the sick and organise the quarantine. Over the months, through 1665 and into the autumn of 1666, about 250 people died, including Mompesson's wife, but the heroic efforts of the village were successful and the epidemic did not spread outside Eyam.

Some of the story has surely been embellished in the telling, but the essential details are recorded in the parish register, among the gravestones around St Lawrence's Church and on nearby cottages. Towns such as Derby and Chesterfield probably suffered worse epidemics of bubonic plague; Eyam has kept its unique place in history because you can stand beside victims' homes, read about their lives and look across to their graves.

Eyam today is neither a sad place nor dwelling in the past. It stands on the hill brow between Middleton Dale and Eyam Moor, as self-contained and aloof as ever. Visitors are impressed by the fine Saxon cross in St Lawrence's churchyard and come to enjoy the traditional well dressing and the sheep roast. But folk-memories of the plague still send a shiver down the spine.

HADDON HALL MAP REF SK2366

Close your eyes and imagine a rambling family castle, built with style, English to the core, unchanged for centuries, full of ghosts, set among trees and pastures above a clear meandering river. What you have in mind is probably Haddon Hall. It is the single most impressive and authentic building in the Peak District, the one that turns historians into poets. Why is this? The simple explanation is that it is a perfectly proportioned medieval manor house, which has been hardly touched since the 16th century. The rest is down to its history, romantic atmosphere and imagination.

Haddon Hall was originally owned by the Vernon family from 1170 until 1567; it came to them by marriage and passed to the Manners family in the same way. Over all those years the house was extended gradually; the Peveril Tower in the 12th century, the cross-wing in the 14th, battlements in the 15th, a gatehouse and courtyard in the 16th and the Long Gallery early in the 17th century. But after that Haddon Hall was left to slumber while the Manners family moved to the magnificent Belvoir Castle as Dukes of Rutland.

Thus the house escaped the fickle architectural fashions of the 18th and 19th centuries, but it was not neglected – it was meticulously maintained, so that when the 9th Duke (then the Marquis of Granby) began his restoration of Haddon in the early 20th century, his task was by no means daunting. The duke ensured that as much as possible of the original structure should be preserved, and that any replacements were carried out to the highest standards. Today Haddon Hall reflects a sense of history that can only come from remaining in the same family for over 800 years. Whether Dorothy Vernon really did escape down the long staircase, out from the chapel to the packhorse bridge to elope with her lover John Manners in 1558, is open to question, but perfectly in keeping with the romance of the place.

Insight & Visit

HERALDIC BEASTS

Important and aristocratic families always had their own ancestral emblems or devices, which accounts for the curious animal shapes that appear on the gutters and in the ironwork of Haddon Hall. The boar emblem represents the Vernon family and the peacock the Manners family; they appear together all over the estate, most spectacularly as carefully clipped and maintained topiary figures in the huge yew bushes outside the gardener's cottage.

Miller's Dale

The walk starts in Tideswell Dale, takes in Miller's Dale, passes Litton Mill and continues into Water-cum-Jolly Dale to follow the River Wye.

Route Directions

1 Follow the path southwards from beside the car park's toilet block into Tideswell Dale, taking the right-hand fork to cross over the little bridge.

2 On entering Miller's Dale, go left along the tarmac lane and continue to Litton Mill. Go

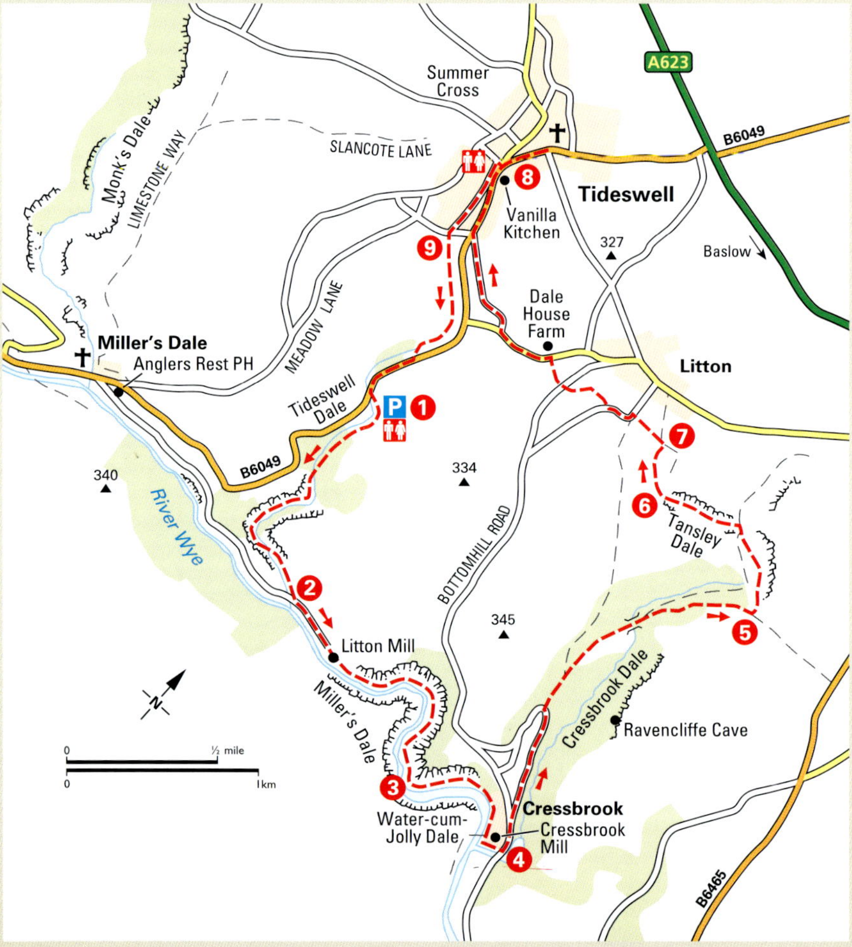

through the gateposts on to a concessionary path through the mill yard. Beyond the mill, the path follows the River Wye, as it meanders through the tight, steep-sided dale.

3 The river widens out in Water-cum-Jolly Dale and the path, liable to flooding here, traces a wall of limestone cliffs before reaching Cressbrook. Do not cross the bridge on the right, but turn left to pass in front of Cressbrook Mill and out on to the road.

4 Turn left along the road, then take the right fork which climbs steadily into Cressbrook Dale. Where the road doubles back uphill leave it for a track going straight ahead into the woods. Beyond a gate the track becomes a narrow path that emerges in a clearing high above the stream. Follow it downhill to a footbridge over the stream, then take the right fork path, which climbs high up the valley side to a stile in the top wall.

5 Don't cross the stile, take the downhill path to the dale bottom, where there's a junction of paths. The one wanted here recrosses the stream on stepping stones, and climbs into Tansley Dale.

6 The path turns right at the top of the dale, and follows a tumbledown wall before crossing it on a step stile. Head for a wall corner in the next field, then veer right through a narrow enclosure to reach a walled track just south of Litton village.

7 Turn left along the track, which comes out onto a country lane at the crown of a sharp bend. Keep straight on down the lane but leave it at the next bend for a well-defined cross-field path to Bottomhill Road. Across the road, a further field path descends to a road at Dale House Farm. Turn left along the pavement, then right on a narrow lane marked 'unsuitable for motor traffic', into Tideswell.

8 After looking around the village head south down the main street, then right on to Gordon Road, which then heads south.

9 Where this ends, continue down the stony track ahead, which runs parallel with the main road. At the far end, take the gated footpath on the left, down to the road into Tideswell Dale. Turn right along the road, back to the car park.

Route facts

DISTANCE/TIME 6 miles (9.7km) 4h

MAP OS Explorer OL24 White Peak

START Tideswell Dale pay car park, grid ref SK 154743

TRACKS Well-defined paths and tracks, path in Water-cum-Jolly Dale liable to flooding, several stiles

GETTING TO THE START
Tideswell is just south of the A623 between Chapel-en-le-Frith and Baslow. Look for the 'Cathedral of the Peak' brown tourist signs. Pass through Tideswell and continue downhill, bending right into Tideswell Dale. The car park (well signed) is nearly a mile (1.6km) south.

THE PUB The George Hotel, Commercial Road, Tideswell.
Tel: 01298 871382; www.georgehoteltideswell.co.uk

❗ There is a particularly steep section of the route in Point 4. We recommend that families with young children avoid this by remaining on the valley-floor path. If the River Wye is running high and brown then the route will be impassable at Water-cum-Jolly Dale, Point 3.

Through Monsal Dale

From Ashford's streets the route climbs to high pastures and one of Derbyshire's best-known viewpoints, where the Monsal Viaduct spans the gorge. The walk continues over the viaduct, descends to Monsal Dale to the River Wye, and follows it westwards through woodland to eventually return to Ashford.

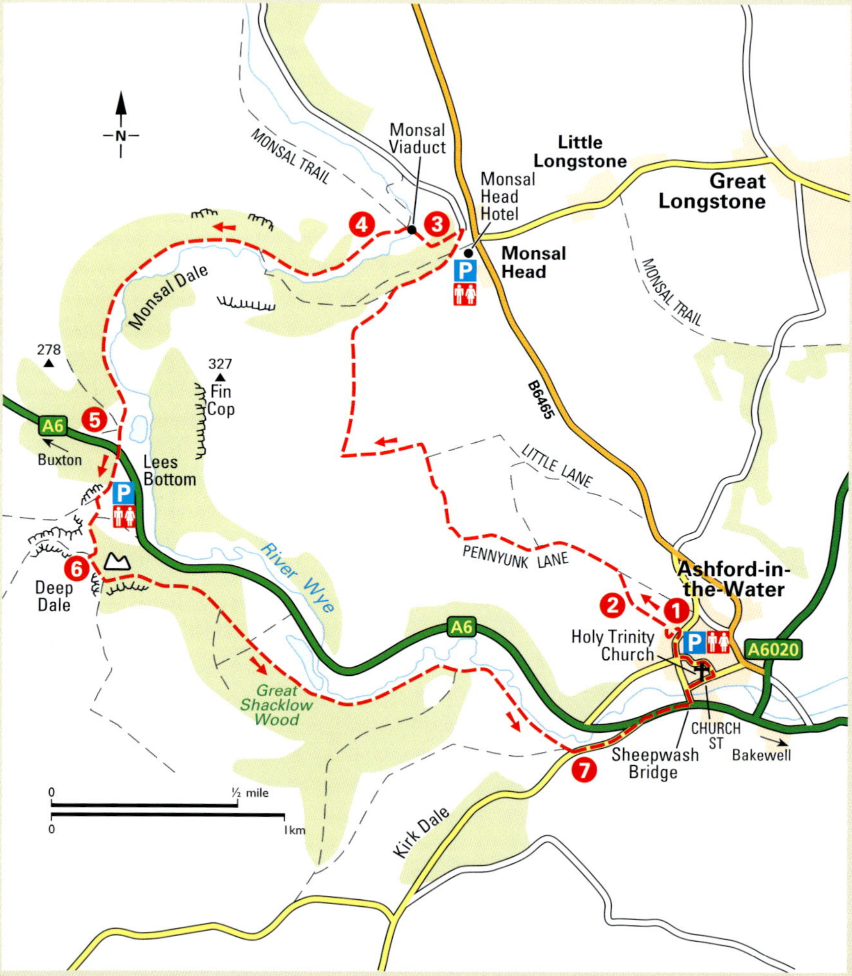

Route Directions

1 From Ashford-in-the-Water car park, walk out to the road and turn right to walk along Vicarage Lane. After 100yds (91m), a footpath on the left doubles back left, then swings sharp right to continue along a ginnel behind a row of houses. Beyond a stile the path enters a field.

2 Head for a stile in the top left corner, then veer slightly right to locate a stile allowing the route to go on to Pennyunk Lane. This walled stony track winds among high pastures. At its end go left uphill along a field-edge. At the top it joins another track, heading north (right) towards the rim of Monsal Dale. The path runs along the top edge of the deep wooded dale to reach the car park at Monsal Head.

3 Take the path marked 'Viaduct and Monsal Trail' here – this way you get to walk across the viaduct. On the other side of the viaduct go through a gate on the left. Ignore the path climbing west up the hillside, but descend southwest on a grassy path raking through scrub woods down into the valley. This shouldn't be confused with the steep eroded path plummeting straight down to the foot of the viaduct.

4 Now you walk down the pleasant valley. The right of way is well away from the river at first but most walkers trace the river bank to emerge at Lees Bottom and a roadside stile.

5 Cross the A6 with great care and go through the White Lodge car park on the path the other side, where the route back to Ashford begins. Beyond the gate carry on along the path, ignoring the turning to Toddington. Go over a wall stile and then up to a rocky path, forking left for the path into Great Shacklow Wood, signposted 'Ashford'.

6 The path now climbs steeply through the trees and stony ground to another gate. Ignore the turning right for Sheldon and continue straight ahead, following a fine ledge path along the steep wooded slopes. Eventually the path comes down to the river, past an old mill, before joining a minor road at the bottom of Kirk Dale.

7 Turn left along the road, down to the A6 and turn right towards Ashford. Leave the road to cross Sheepwash Bridge. Turn right along Church Street, then left along Court Lane to the car park.

Route facts

DISTANCE/TIME 5.5 miles (8.8km) 3h30

MAP OS Explorer OL24 White Peak

START Ashford-in-the-Water car park, grid ref SK 194696

TRACKS Well-defined paths and tracks throughout, 17 stiles and gates

GETTING TO THE START Ashford-in-the-Water is signposted off the main A6 road a few miles northwest of Bakewell. In the village, pass The Bull's Head pub on your right and take Court Lane, the next narrow road on the right, to the car park.

THE PUB The Bull's Head, Ashford-in-the-Water. Tel: 01629 812931

! Parents should keep a close eye on children whilst in the vicinity of the Monsal Head Viaduct. There's a short, steady climb in Point 5. Take care crossing the A6.

LATHKILL DALE

MAP REF SK1865

The classic farmscape of silver-green pastures criss-crossed by drystone walls is dramatically disrupted on the White Peak plateau by the Derbyshire Dales, a series of steep-sided valleys in the limestone. The best dales are gathered together to form a National Nature Reserve, and the jewel in the crown is Lathkill Dale, which runs eastwards from the village of Monyash to the River Wye below Haddon. Access to Lathkill Dale is from Monyash or Over Haddon, 2 miles (3.2km) southwest of Bakewell.

From the west the dale starts out dry, but between Ricklow and Cales Dale the River Lathkill rises out of a cave and soon broadens out into a beautiful, crystal-clear stream, the haunt of water voles and dippers.

Unlike the pasture and silage fields of the plateau, the grassland of the dale is ablaze with wild flowers. The rabbit-cropped south-facing slopes sparkle with rockrose and trefoil, which attract blue butterflies and burnet and forester moths. The shaded herbage of the north-facing slopes is the habitat for one of the Dales' specialities, Jacob's ladder. Further down the Lathkill, following the now well-worn footpath towards Over Haddon, grassland gives way to scrub and to ash woodland that, in the early summer particularly, casts a translucent shade and is full of songbirds.

Lathkill Dale may look untouched, but for many centuries it was mined for lead. The shafts, drainage channels and spoil-heaps have been absorbed into the natural landscape to such an extent that they really enhance its natural beauty. Most of the lead had been exhausted by the 18th century but in the 1840s there was a grandiose attempt to drain the deep mines by building a steam engine, powered by a huge waterwheel fed by the Mandale viaduct. The scheme was, unfortunately, a disaster, as was the Over Haddon gold rush of 1894.

MILLER'S DALE MAP REF SK1473

The River Wye rises at Buxton but then flows east to dissect the limestone plateau. Each reach of the river has its own character, and each section of the narrow valley or dale has its own name. Thus Wye Dale turns into Chee Dale, which gives way to Miller's Dale, then Water-cum-Jolly Dale and Monsal Dale. They are names to çonjure with and to stir the imagination.

The presence of the river is a unifying theme; it brought welcome industry to the outback in the days of the Industrial Revolution and around this industry the little settlement of Miller's Dale grew up, squeezed awkwardly into the narrow valley of the Wye. Here lived the rail men and quarry workers and their families, and there was even a station, but all of that is gone now and the industrial areas are returning to nature.

In many respects Miller's Dale, to either side of Litton Mill, is the most impressive and complete dale to visit. Not only does the Wye negotiate a barrage of natural obstacles here, side-stepping hills, twisting through gaps and gorges and rock faces, but also there are mill races and weirs where the power of the water has been diverted to drive 19th-century cotton mills (Litton and Cressbrook, a little way further downstream). A recreational footpath, the Monsal Trail, runs the length of the dale, allowing access to the old mill yards (some of the buildings are still in use, but not for weaving). There are footbridges at either end of Miller's Dale allowing access to convenient car parks.

Several side dales run north from the main valley, often dry and grassy but sometimes decked with ash woodland and with a stream dancing down to meet the Wye. The most attractive are Cressbrook Dale, the best for wildlife and with some beautiful ash woodland, Tideswell Dale, with access to the village of Tideswell, and Monks Dale, close to the village of Wormhill. Wormhill belies its name by being an attractive scatter of old farmhouses, with a village green, stocks and a fountain/well (dressed in August) commemorating James Brindley, the famous canal engineer, who was born close by at Tunstead.

PEAK FOREST MAP REF SK1179

High, wide and windswept, it is rather hard to believe that this landscape of sheep pasture was once a royal chase – the Forest in the Peak – or that its administrative capital was this little village. For about a century, until the relaxation of the Forest Laws in 1250, kings and princes used the vast expanse of woodland and heath between the Goyt and the Derwent rivers as a private playground; they hunted wild boar and roe deer and stayed at the recently built Peveril Castle, which stands high above Castleton to the northeast.

By Elizabethan times most of the ancient woodland had disappeared, but what remained of the wilderness was fenced in as a deer park. A Steward and five Royal Foresters managed the enclosure system and had premises in the Chamber, a building on the site of the present Chamber Farm. Swainmotes, or forest courts, settled any disputes. It was the foresters' task to care for the deer, by controlling grazing, by preventing walls from being built and by keeping people out. The deer increased fourfold, but this was only a temporary triumph. Around 1655 the land was allocated to the Dukes of Devonshire and was officially deforested, though the last of the trees had already been felled to provide pit props for the coal mines on Combs Moss. Scrub and heath took over the countryside until the turn of the 19th century.

The Chamber of the Peak, and the few cottages that made up the village of Peak Forest, had been the heart of the royal forest, but had not stood among trees; this part of the limestone plateau was called the Great Pasture and was used for sheep, as it is now. The present village of stone-built houses and farms grew up around a church built by the Dowager Duchess of Devonshire when the land was first acquired. This was at the time of the Commonwealth and could only be construed as an act of defiance when considering its dedication – to 'King Charles, King and Martyr'.

Considering its colourful past, Peak Forest is a modest little place. A post office and pub (The Devonshire Arms of course) cater for any secular needs.

STANTON IN PEAK

MAP REF SK2464

Important ritual landscapes, stretches of countryside that were set aside in prehistoric times because of their spiritual significance, are not confined to Stonehenge and the Dorset Cercus. Apart from megaliths and barrows, such places often retain traces of avenues and earth banks, dykes and cairns. They draw the eye from miles around, dominating the high ground and casting a powerful spell on everyone from archaeologists to New Age travellers. They ask so many questions of our modern culture that they are as uncomfortable as they are fascinating. Such a place is Stanton Moor.

Stanton village is a ribbon of cottages on a steep and winding side road, built out of the limestone and below the brow of the gritstone, sheltered from the moor by old quarries and a swathe of tall sweet-chestnut trees. The initials WPT, carved into the lintels of many doorways, refer to William Thornhill, who built most of the village in the 1830s and whose family lived at Stanton Hall. The 18th-century Flying Childers Inn celebrates the greatest racehorse of its day, trained by Sir Hugh Childers for the 4th Duke of Devonshire. Opposite the inn is Holly House that still has half of its windows still blocked up to avoid the 1697 window tax.

Birchover Lane, running south of Stanton, follows the western edge of the moor. Parking places give access to pathways through birch scrub and over heather and bilberry to the Bronze Age landscape. About 70 barrows or burial cairns have been identified on the small island of gritstone. The biggest, covering the site of twelve cremations, still stands 5 feet (1.5m) tall, inside a double ring of stones with an outer diameter of 54 feet (16.4m). There are three stone circles or monuments on Stanton Moor, the most famous is the Nine Ladies. Outside this stone ring, about 100 feet (30.5m) to the south, stands the solitary King Stone, which is part of the ritual site. The story goes that a fiddler and nine maidens were turned to stone for dancing on Sunday. This is a typical example of prehistoric culture being Christianised.

Activity

WYE VALLEY VIEWPOINT

Pilhough Lane, going northeast out of Stanton, makes a pleasant walk or drive because of its superb views over the Wye Valley and Haddon Hall. Before the church was built parishioners had to walk this way to Rowsley, and the Thornhill family had a viewing platform, called the Stand or Belvedere, set into the steep edge so that people could stop and rest and also enjoy the prospect.

Visit

ROCKING STONES

Many of the sandstone outcrops that rise out of the bracken between Stanton and Elton have historical associations. Rowtor Rocks, near Birchover and overlooking the Druid Inn, was famous for its Rocking Stones, but the best of these is a 50-ton block on a sandstone pivot. Unfortunately, it was vandalised in 1799 and no longer moves. At the foot of nearby Cratcliff Rocks is a hermit's cave, once the abode of a rabbit-catcher.

Bakewell and the Monsal Trail

An easy ride from the town of Bakewell, with its railway heritage, which loops through a picturesque limestone village and riverside hay meadows.

Route Directions

1 Access to the trackbed is via the gap at the left side of the imposing structure. Turn left along the level track, a compacted and well-surfaced route which, beyond some industrial units that occupy the former goods yard, runs initially through thin woods. Passing beneath the main road, Bakewell is left behind and soon Hassop Old Station comes into view.

2 The station buildings have largely gone, although an old warehouse has now been converted. Beyond here, the trees thin and become less constricting, and fine views to the hill slopes climbing towards Longstone Edge draw the eye. There's an abundance of wild flowers along this section during spring and summer. The old trackbed passes under and over several roads and lanes before reaching the rather impressive buildings at Great Longstone's old station. The station partially retains its canopy, while next door is one of the buildings of the Thornbridge Estate.

3 Note the sign that warns you that there is no exit for cyclists beyond this point, however it is worth cycling 0.25 mile (400m) to the end of the useable track for some great views across towards the River Wye in its deep valley. You can choose here to simply retrace your route back to Bakewell, a distance of 5.25 miles (8.4km). Another option, though, is to return to Great Longstone Station and take the steep flight of steps, left, to a minor road. Turn left along this road for an easy, level ride to the village centre at Great Longstone.

4 At the market cross and village green, fork right along either of the lanes. Both wind down to the main street, lined with fine limestone cottages and houses, to reach The White Lion. Just beyond this, take Church Lane, left, to rise up a gentle hill to the parish church. The road bends to the right here, so beginning an undulating, but fairly easy ride along this narrow road, named Beggarway Lane, offering great views up to Longstone Edge and odd glimpses back towards the buildings of Bakewell.

5 In approximately 0.75 miles (1.2km), turn right along the lane that leaves at a left-hand bend. Longreave Lane is an easy downhill coast for nearly a mile (1.6km) that eventually reaches a road junction at a railway overbridge. Fork left here just before the bridge, up

Route facts

DISTANCE/TIME 8 miles (12.9km) 3h

MAP OS Explorer OL24 White Peak

START Bakewell Old Station, grid ref SK 223690

TRACKS Old railway trackbed and back lanes

GETTING TO THE START Bakewell's old railway station is located on Station Road – the road that forks off to the right at the memorial as you take the A619 road for Baslow out of the town centre and cross the bridge over the Wye. There's ample parking at the old station.

CYCLE HIRE None nearby

THE PUB The White Lion, Great Longstone. Tel: 01629 640252

❶ One short climb, one long downhill stretch.

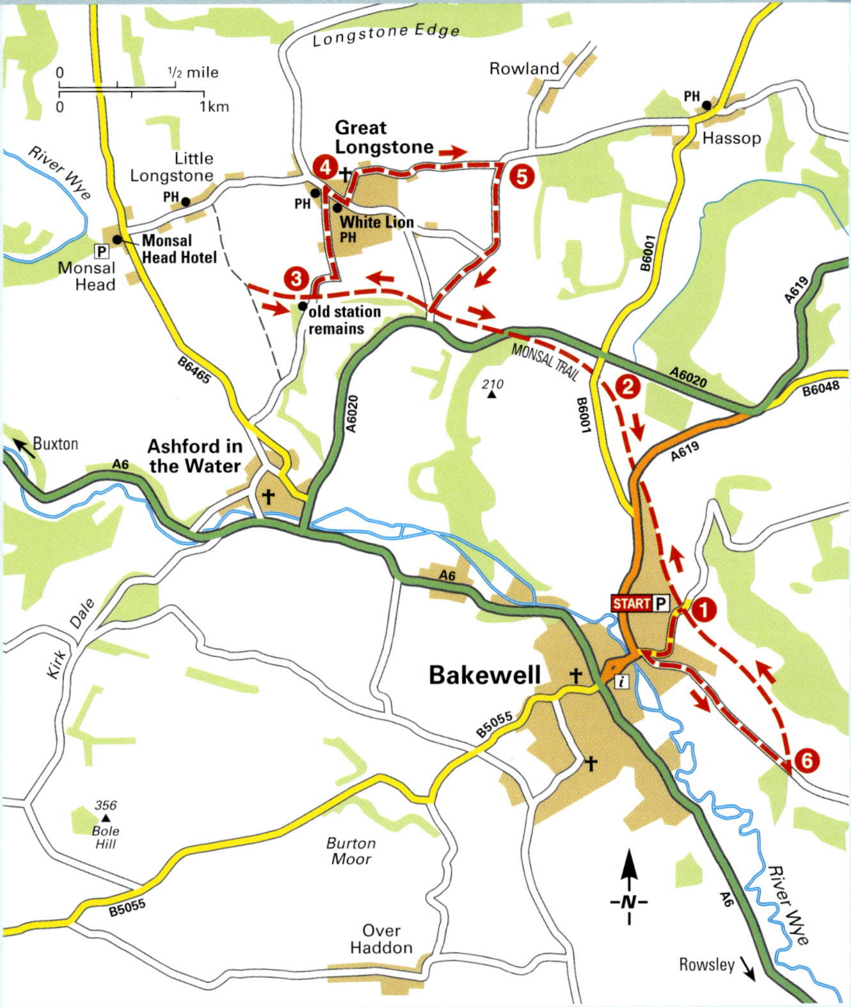

a gravelly ramp to regain the old railway. Turn left here to return to Bakewell. To extend the route you can now cycle across the car park and take Station Road downhill (take care by the parked cars). At the junction at the bottom of the road turn sharp left along Coombs Road, passing the car park entrance. This peaceful, level lane runs for about a mile (1.6km), amid pastures and hay meadows to eventually reach a high-arched viaduct crossing.

6 Immediately before the viaduct, look for the Monsal Trail board, left, indicating a short, sharp incline, up which you wheel your bicycle to the old railway. Turn left to return to Bakewell and enjoy the good views across the town.

TIDESWELL MAP REF SK1575

Daniel Defoe, searching for the famous 'Seven Wonders of the Peak' in 1726, was not impressed by the ebbing and flowing well he viewed in a garden of Manchester Road in Tideswell. This may have been because he was looking at the wrong well (the original 'Wonder' was probably at Barmoor Clough), but in any case the water no longer ebbs and flows with the tide, and Tideswell got its name from an ancient British chieftain called Tidi. This is not to say that wells were not important in the village; it lies at the 1,000-foot (304m) contour on the limestone plateau, set in a dry bowl amid a grey cobwebbing of walls and wind-scorched fields. In fact, Tideswell is renowned for the quality of its well-dressing ceremony, which starts the Wakes Week on the Saturday nearest Saint John the Baptist's Day (24 June); the week's festivities are concluded with a traditional torchlight procession and a unique Morris Dance.

In the 14th century Tideswell was a thriving place, confident in the future of the wool trade and lead mining. The parish church, dedicated to Saint John the Baptist, reflected this optimism; it was built in just 75 years and was a classic cruciform shape, of Decorated and Perpendicular styles, spacious and with superb fittings, carvings and brasses. That Tideswell dwindled to a village was in some ways a stroke of luck, particularly as the glorious church, often described as the 'Cathedral of the Peak', was bypassed by rich patrons and Victorian megalomaniacs, and stands today in splendid unaltered isolation. Around the church, the largest in the area, run lawns and railings separating it from the more prosaic buildings at the heart of the village.

Two of Tideswell's renowned musical forefathers are buried in the church: 'the Minstrel of the Peak', William Newton, who died in 1830, and Samuel Slack, who died in 1822. Slack, whose name bore no relation to his vocal chords, was famous for two things: singing for George III and for stopping a bull dead in its tracks by bellowing at it. His voice, apparently, could be heard a mile (1.6km) away.

Insight

TIDESWELL CROSSES

In the 15th century all the roads around Tideswell were marked by stone crosses. Unfortunately, only one of these survives intact, at Wheston to the west, close to the 17th-century hall; the rest just exist in fragments, their water-filled bases built into walls and gateposts. A local tradition is to float a cross made of grass blades on the water and make a wish.

Insight

THE SEVEN WONDERS OF THE PEAK

The 'Seven Wonders of the Peak' first appeared in print in 1622 in a set of poems by Michael Drayton. His list included Peak Cavern, Poole's Cavern, Eldon Hole, St Ann's Well, the ebbing and flowing well at Tideswell, Mam Tor and Peak Forest. Some years later Thomas Hobbes wrote a poem also including Seven Wonders, but substituting Chatsworth House for Peak Forest. It was left to the redoubtable traveller, Daniel Defoe, in his tour of 1726, to debunk the myth of the wonders – including the singularly unimpressive well at Tideswell.

To the east of Tideswell is the little village of Litton, a pretty gathering of 18th-century cottages beside a green with a set of stocks close to the Red Lion pub. Tideswell Dale and Cressbrook Dale run south, from west and east of the village, beautiful in their own right and giving access to Miller's Dale.

WINSTER MAP REF SK2460

Midway between the sleepy little villages of Elton and Wensley (which has its own Wensley Dale, but without the cheese) rests the sleepy little village of Winster. People go to Winster because they intend to, as it lies off the main tourist routes, though close enough to Matlock to make use of its shops and services. Most of the attraction of Winster is its characterful history, as one of the old lead-mining centres with 18th-century houses lining the main street between a fine 17th-century Dower House (now a hotel) and a 15th- to 16th-century Market House. The latter is matchbox-sized and a delightful structure of weathered stone arches, once open but now bricked in to keep it all standing, and an upper floor of brick, which may have replaced its earlier timbers. The National Trust bought the Market House in 1906, its first acquisition in the Peaks, and part of it houses an Information Centre. Close by is Winster Hall, an early Georgian house said to be haunted.

Winster used to be full of alehouses; witness the name Shoulder of Mutton, carved by the door of what is now a private house on West Bank. At the top of the bank, just out of the village, is the still-thriving Miners Standard, which has on display some of the old lead-mining equipment. It is here that the traditional Winster Morris perform their dances at the start of Wakes Week in June each year; a procession then leads through the village, finishing up at the Miners Standard for refreshment.

A more recent tradition is that of pancake races on Shrove Tuesday. It began as light-hearted fun, organised by the local headmaster as a diversion during wartime for the children, but has now become a more serious – but still fun – affair, with secret race training and stringent rules about making the batter.

Activity

A HERMIT'S CAVE NEAR ELTON

West of Winster is the old lead-mining village of Elton. A popular walk heading north from the village leads to a small medieval hermit's cave at Cratcliffe Rocks – carved into the cave is a crucifix. An unusual rock formation known as Robin Hood's Stride and a stone circle are also seen on this walk of about 4 miles (6.4km).

Visit

CRESSBROOK DALE

Cressbrook Dale, just to the south of Tideswell, is part of the Derbyshire Dales National Nature Reserve. You may see wild orchids, cranesbill, mountain pansy, globeflower and spring sandwort growing on the limestone grassland in abundance. One of the many alkaline-loving plants is the Nottingham catchfly, which loves dry, stony places. The white flowers roll back in daytime, but are fragrant at night with perfume designed to attract pollinating moths.

NEAR BAKEWELL

Visit

ARBOR LOW'S ANCIENT STONES

Three miles (4.8km) along the Long Rake west of Youlgreave, off the road to the left and accessible from a car park, is the famous henge of Arbor Low, probably built by the Beaker People in around 2000 BC. The whole monument, with rock-cut ditch, bank and a circle of 47 stones, measures 250 feet (76.2m) across. Although the massive stone blocks are all lying flat and half buried, Arbor Low is still a powerful place, especially in winter sunlight.

Insight

DEW PONDS

Dew ponds are a feature of limestone pastures in the White Peak. Because the underlying rock is porous there are no natural pools, so farmers have created their own, filled by rain, mists, dew and hosepipes.

YOULGREAVE

MAP REF SK2064

A long, handsome village on the shoulder of Bradford Dale, Youlgreave (known as Pommie by most locals) has one of the most elaborate well-dressing ceremonies in the Peak District, taking place at Midsummer each year, when five wells are dressed with biblical scenes. The White Peak tradition has its roots in the days when wells were essential and were blessed to give thanks for water. However, in the case of Youlgreave, the records only go back to 1829, coinciding with the provision of the village's own public water supply via a conduit from the Dale below. The water was gathered in a huge circular stone tank called The Fountain, which stands in the middle of the village. Nearby, on the opposite side of the street, is the Co-op building, which once had a vital role in the social survival of the area but is now a youth hostel.

On the east side of Youlgreave, by the road which then sweeps down to Alport, stands All Saints Church, described by experts as one of the most impressive churches in Derbyshire. Essentially Norman and with an unusually broad nave, the most obvious feature of All Saints is its 14th-century tower, chunky and stylish in the best Perpendicular tradition. Inside are sturdy columns and a 13th-century font, unique in that it has two bowls, and the fine monuments include a tiny effigy of Thomas Cokayne, who died in 1488. The church was restored in 1870 and has stained-glass windows by Burne-Jones and Kempe.

Three bridges cross the River Bradford below Youlgreave, including a clapper bridge of stone slabs and a packhorse bridge, which is now used as a footbridge. The short walk to the confluence with the Lathkill is popular, but by turning southeast, over the main bridge and on to the Limestone Way, you can explore the fine countryside towards Birchover, past the Iron Age hill-fort of Castle Hill and the Nine Stones Close Circle (four stones are still standing tall), to the great tumbling rock tors of Robin Hood's Stride (once known as Mock Beggars Hall), Cratcliffe Rocks and Rowtor Rocks. Pagan myths, hermits' caves and a popular dining pub, the Druid Inn, are among the attractions of this magical corner of the Peak.

YOULGREAVE

TOURIST INFORMATION CENTRE

Bakewell
The Old Market Hall,
Bridge Street.
Tel: 01629 816558

PLACES OF INTEREST

Arbor Low Stone Circle
Upper Oldhams Farm,
Monyash.

Cascades Gardens
Bonsall.
Tel: 01629 822813;
www.derbyshiregarden.com
Some 4 acres (1.6ha) of themed gardens.

Eyam Hall
Tel: 01433 631976;
www.eyamhall.com
The furniture, portraits and other items at the Hall reflect the fact that this is still a family home and has been for centuries. Also home to a craft centre.

Eyam Museum
Tel: 01433 631371; www.eyammuseum.demon.co.uk
The museum tells the story of the bubonic plague, how it reached Eyam and was contained there.

Haddon Hall
Bakewell.
Tel: 01629 812855;
www.haddonhall.co.uk
A splendid house that has remained virtually untouched by the passage of time. Topiary gardens.

Old House Museum
Bakewell.
Tel: 01629 813642;
www.oldhousemuseum.hammerdesign.co.uk
This Tudor house is home to a folk museum and a Victorian kitchen; toys and lace are among the exhibits.

Stanton Moor
Nine Ladies Stone Circle.

Winster Market House
Winster, 4 miles (6.4km) west of Matlock.
Tel: 01335 350503;
www.nationaltrust.org.uk
Restored by the National Trust, the Market House is now used as an information centre. The building dates back to the late 17th/early 18th century. Free.

SHOPPING

Bakewell
Market on Mon, includes cattle, except Bank Holiday Mon when a general market is held.

LOCAL SPECIALITIES

Bakewell Puddings
Original Bakewell Pudding Shop, The Square, Bakewell.
Tel: 01629 812193; www.bakewellpuddingshop.co.uk
Bloomers Original Bakewell Puddings, Water Lane, Bakewell.
Tel: 01629 814844

General Foodstuffs
Bakewell Farmers Market, last Sat of month.
Foods from The Chatsworth Estate, Chatsworth Farm Shop, Stud Farm, Pilsley, Bakewell.
Tel: 01246 583392

Meats
New Close Farm Shop, Over Haddon, Bakewell.
Tel: 01629 814280;
www.newclosefarm.com
Home cured pork, bacon and cooked meats.

Pork Pies
Connoisseurs Deli, Water Street, Water Lane, Bakewell.
Tel: 01629 812044

SPORTS & ACTIVITIES

GUIDED WALKS

Bakewell & Peak District
Professional Blue Badge Guides can arrange walks for individuals or for parties.
Tel: 01629 534284.

Derbyshire Dales Countryside Service
Planning and Development Services, Town Hall, Matlock.
Full guided walks service.
Tel: 01629 761326 for details.

National Park Walks with a Ranger
For more details contact the Peak District National Park.
Tel: 01629 816200;
www.peakdistrict.gov.uk

Annual Peak District Walking Festival
Large programme of guided walks in late Apr/early May.
Tel: 0870 444 7275; www.visitpeakdistrict.com/walk

Peak Walking Adentures
Tel: 07870 778585;
www.peakwalking.com

HANG GLIDING

Bradwell
Derbyshire Flying Centre.
Tel: 0845 108 1577;
www.d-f-c.co.uk

HORSE-RIDING

Haddon House Riding Stables
Over Haddon, Bakewell.
Tel: 01629 813723; www.haddonhousestables.co.uk

LONG-DISTANCE FOOTPATHS & TRAILS

The Limestone Way
A 46-mile (74km) route south from Castleton through the White Peak to Rocester (Staffordshire).

The Midshires Way
Stretches 223 miles (360km) from Stockport to Buckinghamshire via the White Peak.

The Monsal Trail
Runs for 8.5 miles (13.7km) from Blackwell Mill Junction near Buxton to Coombs Viaduct near Bakewell.

NAVIGATION
Tideswell.
Tel: 01298 872470; www.silvanavigationschool.com
Map and compass training.

ANNUAL EVENTS & CUSTOMS

For the full programme visit www.visitpeakdistrict.com

Ashford in the Water
Well dressing, late May to early Jun.
Blessing of the Wells Trinity Sunday, May.

Bakewell
Well dressing, late Jun/early Jul.
Carnival, early Jul.
Bakewell Show, early Aug.

Bradwell
Well dressing, early Aug.

Eyam
Well dressing and demonstration late Aug.
Plague Commemoration Service, last Sunday in Aug.
Carnival, Aug/Sep.

Flagg
Point-to-Point races, first Tue after Easter.

Little Longstone
Well-dressing and demonstration mid-Jul.

Litton
Well-dressing demonstration, mid-Jun.
Well-dressing, late Jun/early Jul.
Litton Horticultural Show, early Sep.

Middleton by Youlgreave
Well-dressing demonstration, late May.
Well-dressing, late May/early Jun.

Monyash
Well-dressing demonstration, late May.
Well-dressing, late May/early Jun.
Antiques and Collectors' Fair, late Aug.

Pilsley
Well-dressing, mid- to late Jul.

Stoney Middleton
Well-dressing, late Jul.

Tideswell
Wakes Week, late Jun.
Well-dressing, late Jun/early Jul.
Male Voice Choir and Silver Band Annual Concert, early Jul.

Winster
Pancake racing, Shrove Tuesday.
Winster Wakes Festivities, late Jun/early Jul.

Wormhill
Well-dressing and demonstration, late Aug.

Youlgreave
Well-dressing, late Jun.

Tea Rooms

The Original Bakewell Pudding Shop

The Square, Bakewell, Derbyshire DE45 1BT
Tel: 01629 812193; www.bakewellpuddingshop.co.uk

Above the shop where Bakewell's famed recipe was re-created, this comfortable tea room has exposed beams reminiscent of a medieval barn. Indulge in sandwiches and pastries, afternoon tea to a more filling meal, but don't miss out on a generous helping of Bakewell Pudding.

The Old Smithy Tea Rooms

Church Street, Monyash, Derbyshire DE45 1JH
Tel: 01629 810190; www.oldsmithymonyash.pizco.com

Set beside the village green and ancient cross, the Old Smithy provides supremely well for walkers and visitors to this delightful old village. Although renowned for its all-day breakfast, traditional cream teas and pastries are its main draws.

Eyam Tea Rooms

The Square, Eyam, Derbyshire S32 5RB
Tel: 01433 631274

At the Town End part of Eyam and overlooking the pretty square this tea room has a particular reputation for fine home-made cakes, gateaux and scones. There's also a good choice of vegetarian meals and snacks.

Monsal View Café

Monsal Head, Ashford in the Water, Derbyshire DE45 1NL
Tel: 01629 640346

Overlooking magnificent Monsal Dale this friendly, stone-floored café with a roaring fire in winter offers filling fare, from snacks to restaurant meals and Derbyshire cream teas.

Pubs

The Red Lion

Litton, near Tideswell, Derbyshire SK17 8QU
Tel: 01298 871458

Tiny beamed rooms, uneven stone floors and glowing logs in the hearths make this inn a magnet for pub aficionados. A friendly landlady, affable locals, great microbrewery beers and a very tasty menu make it one of the best in the Peak District.

The Lathkil Hotel

Over Haddon, Bakewell, Derbyshire DE45 1JE
Tel: 01629 812501; www.lathkil.co.uk

This long-established inn was built to serve lead-miners. Today's guests tuck into a mix of simple bar meals, top-notch dishes, and beers from Peak District breweries.

The Bull's Head Inn

Foolow, Derbyshire S32 5QD
Tel: 01433 630873

A row of cottages in a peaceful hamlet forms this classic inn. The cosy interior features beams, flagstone floors, oak panelling, log fires and simple furnishings. To one end there is a smarter dining room; space here, then, for walkers, diners and locals to indulge in beers from the Peaks Ales Brewery with the guarantee of good, filling fodder, including grand Sunday roasts.

The Barrel Inn

Bretton, Eyam, Derbyshire S32 5QD
Tel: 01433 630856; www.thebarrelinn.co.uk

Derbyshire's highest pub, The Barrel Inn stands right on the lip of Eyam Edge, giving immense views across the heart of the White Peak. Expect beers from Hardys and Hansons brewery and good size portions of tasty, but unpretentious pub food, served in comfortable surroundings of antique seats, age-smoothed flagged floors, low beams, country prints and brass plates.

Derwent Valley & Eastern Moors

A ribbon of high gritstone moorland runs all the way from Stocksbridge in the north to Matlock in the south, which serves as a buffer between the industries and suburbs of Sheffield and Chesterfield and the main artery of the Peaks, the River Derwent. At the edge of the heather moors are great shelves of gritstone, etched by ancient ice into a famous series of west-facing cliffs or Edges. At the head of the Derwent there are many attractive villages, all quite different, and several historic houses, of which Chatsworth House stands supreme.

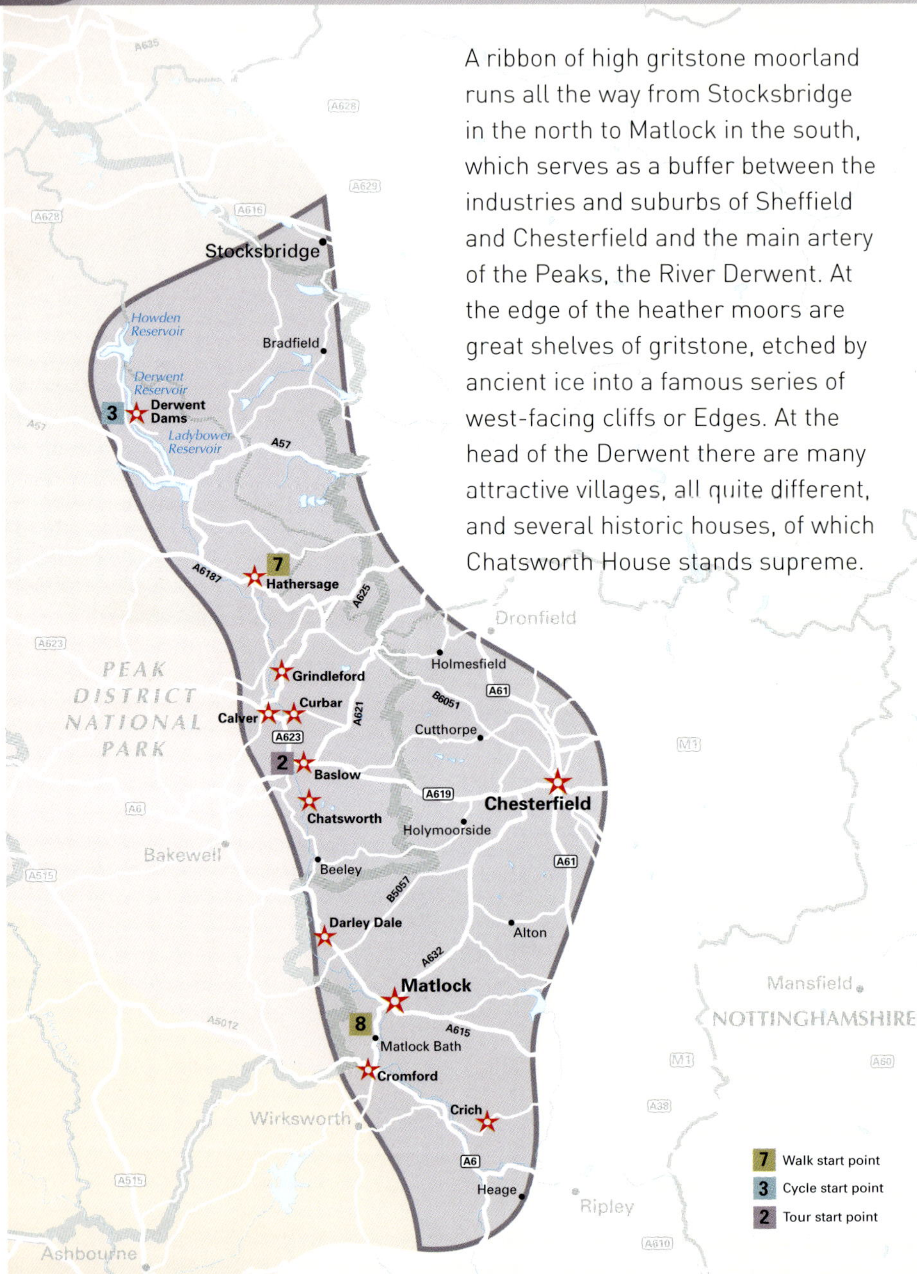

Fletchers

Unmissable attractions

The Derwent flows down from the northern Peak District, watched over by Frogatt, Curbar, Baslow and Stanage, winding through a mellow valley, skirted by woods, meadows and pretty villages. On the river banks is the magnificent Chatsworth House. Joined by the Wye, the Derwent flows through a narrow gorge where the little town of Matlock has been built. Overlooked by the cliffs of the Heights of Abraham, Matlock is a tourist honeypot. Old Matlock is on the east bank of the Derwent, where the turbulent waters are ideal for whitewater rafting and kayaking.

1

2

1 Calver & Curbar
The little village of Calver nestles in the Derwent Valley beneath rugged Curbar Edge, an area popular with both walkers and climbers.

2 Cromford
The waters of Bonsall Brook, a tributary of the River Derwent, were used to power Arkwright's cotton spinning mills.

3 Crich Tramway Village
A fascinating place where visitors can ride on vintage trams, which run from a period street setting into open countryside.

4 Chatsworth House
Standing within superb parkland and fine gardens, Chatsworth House, often known as the 'Palace of the Peak', is a treasure trove of works of art.

BASLOW MAP REF SK2572

The 18th-century turnpike road from Sheffield used to cross the River Derwent next to St Anne's Church in the oldest part of Baslow, called Bridge End. A modern bridge now spans the river a short distance to the south, making it possible to idle about the 17th-century triple-arched bridge and take a closer look at the little toll house (the doorway is just 3.5 feet/1m high) that guards it. Further along the lane on the west bank of the river stands Bubnell Hall, which is as old as the bridge, while on the east bank, above the main road, stands Baslow Hall, an early 20th-century copy that has been converted into the luxurious Fischer's Hotel.

On the far side of Baslow is Nether End, almost a village in itself, gathered around its own little Goose Green and with a row of pretty thatched cottages, which overlook Bar Brook. Thatched cottages are now quite rare in the area, although 'black thatch' (heather or turf) may once have been more widespread. Nether End marks the north entrance to the Chatsworth Estate and there is a touch of sophisticated comfort about everything; this applies equally to the nearby Cavendish Hotel, which contains some fine antiques from Chatsworth.

Further east along the Sheffield road the Bar Brook cuts a nick in the dramatic gritstone scarp, with Baslow Edge on one side and Birchen Edge on the other. A sea of bracken laps the footings of the rock faces, while the moorland above the Edge is a lonely wilderness of heather and the home of merlin and grouse. It was once the home of farmers too, in the Bronze Age, when the climate was a little kinder. It is astonishing to find field systems still visible from more than 3,000 years ago. Below Baslow Bar, just out of Nether End, it is also possible to see narrow fields separated by drystone walls that follow the old reverse-S pattern, the sign of ox-ploughing in medieval times.

CALVER & CURBAR

MAP REF SK2574

The Derwent divides these shrinking communities; Calver on the west bank lies in the lee of the limestone hills, while Curbar sits below a gritstone edge, close to the moors. An bridge built in the 18th century links them, but this is bypassed by a crossing just downstream and most people never notice Curbar as they swing west to Calver Sough.

Calver has an industrial side to its character; shoes and sinks were among its products. The steel sink factory occupies what was once a cotton mill, built by Richard Arkwright in 1805 and employing up to 200 people. The mill's moment of glory came in the 1970s when its satanic profile won it the role of Colditz Castle in a television series.

On the other side of the Derwent, Curbar is a quiet place on the shoulder of pastureland before Curbar Edge. The older features of the village include a circular pinfold or stock-pound, a covered well and circular trough, and a lock-up with a conical roof. These structures survived because they were fashioned in stone and were built to last. In the 18th century nobody could foresee

a time when sheep wouldn't stray, horses wouldn't be thirsty and men wouldn't get drunk.

The old Chesterfield turnpike heads east out of Curbar, seeking the gap in the gritstone edge on the skyline. Great stone slabs were easily won from the Edge and were used in the area for more than just millstones. On the tussocky pasture close to the village lies a small group of gravestones marking the final resting place of the Cundy family, who died of the plague in 1632 (more than 30 years before the Eyam outbreak). Further up, several natural slabs of rock bear biblical references, the work of a molecatcher-cum-preacher, Edwin Gregory, who worked on the Chatsworth Estate a century ago. Finally, as the road straightens and heads southeast over the Bar Brook, there are drystone walls, guideposts and a clapper bridge, dating back to the packhorse era before the road became a turnpike in 1759.

CHATSWORTH

MAP REF SK2670

Towards the end of the 17th century, William Cavendish, the 4th Earl of Devonshire and soon to be made the 1st Duke for his part in putting William of Orange on the throne, decided his house needed a radical new look. For a while he tinkered with alterations, but finally knocked everything down and started again. Demolishing one great historic house to build another might seem an odd investment of a lifetime, but in those days great families were judged by their homes and gardens; fashion and taste was everything.

The Chatsworth House that rose from the rubble of the Elizabethan mansion was of a classical, Palladian style, to the duke's own design. It took about 30 years to complete and it set the seal on his new status – even some of the window frames were gilded on the outside. The irony is that he never saw it at its best. Great houses needed great gardens and grounds, and these took decades to establish. In the middle of the 18th century 'Capability' Brown and James Paine laid the foundations of what we see today by altering the course of the river and roads, building bridges and setting out woodland vistas.

The house is bursting with great works of art in the most superb settings; the Painted Hall is a work of art in itself, with huge, swirling scenes from the life of Julius Caesar by Louis Laguerre on the ceiling and upper part of the walls. Splendour follows splendour as you progress through the house (a tour of about a third of a mile/0.5km), but one of the most engaging features that stays in the memory of visitors long after they have departed is the wonderful *trompe l'oeil* painting of a violin on the inner door of the State Music Room.

None can deny the magnificence of the house itself, but the real secret of Chatsworth is its setting. From any direction it looks majestic, and from the southwest, approaching Edensor on a sunny evening, it can be breathtaking. On the horizon to the east are the high gritstone moors; in the middle distance are tiers of woodland, melting into ribbons and stands of beech and oak and rolling parkland; and in the foreground winds the Derwent. The front of the house reflects the peach-glow of evening sunlight to perfection; around it are superb formal gardens and the fine Emperor fountain. This is a view the 1st Duke could only have dreamed about.

The Chatsworth Estate stretches far and wide and includes grouse moors, working farmland and estate villages. Of the villages Edensor catches the eye first. Until the 1830s the village stood a little closer to the river but the 6th Duke had it moved further back, out of sight. The new houses were a hotchpotch of styles; Italian, Swiss, almost anything but vernacular English. Only one house of the original village remains, called Park Cottage, but known at one time as Naboth's Vineyard. The biblical reference relates to the owner in 1838, who is supposed to have refused to sell or be relocated. Just 1 mile (1.6km) to the northwest lies Pilsley, more compact than Edensor, with the Chatsworth Farm Shop, a pub and a microbrewery.

Just outside the Chatsworth Estate to the south, but within its influence and historic ownership, lies Beeley. This old working village, tucked neatly away and with many of the elements of a much older settlement, has quite a refreshing character. A tannery once stood beside the brook, and there was an estate-built school and a barn to house the coal wagons that supplied the Chatsworth estate glasshouses with fuel. Over the years most of the old buildings have been put to other uses, but fortunately not the public house (The Devonshire Arms), which is still a good excuse for stopping on the way up to the moors.

Visit

CHATSWORTH DEER

The deer at Chatsworth are fallow deer, which were introduced into Britain by the Normans to grace their hunting forests. Fallow differ from the native red and roe deer in having a spotted coat and broad antlers. A visit to Chatsworth's glorious parkland can give the impression of an English version of the African Serengeti, with cattle, sheep and deer instead of wildebeest and impala.

Insight

BILBERRY TIME

Purple bird droppings on moorland walls are a sign that it is bilberry time. Bilberry (blaeberry in Scotland and blueberry in America) grows on the slopes and along the road verges of Beeley Moor. The bell-shaped flowers give way to glorious dark purple berries in July; despite being rather inconspicuous, the fruit bushes are quickly stripped by grouse, foxes and other wild animals. But just 30 minutes of gathering should produce enough fruit for a small pie. The taste is delicious.

Activity

WILDLIFE OF THE MOORLAND

Of all the heather moorland in the Peaks the expanse above Beeley is probably the best for wildlife. This has been due in part to its isolation and lack of access, but now it is possible to explore several of its finest areas without damaging the most sensitive ecological sites. You don't have to walk very far to find the wildlife as the roadside walls are one of the best places to look. Lichen-coloured moths, such as the grey chi and glaucous shears sit on the stone walls, while the full-grown caterpillars of emperor and northern eggar moths like to sun themselves on the tops of bilberry and heather clumps.

The Snow Road

This tour begins at Baslow, in a cleft of the Derwent valley with gritstone cliffs to the east and the White Peak to the west. It heads north to Ladybower Reservoir and then climbs steadily northwest to cross the Dark Peak by the infamous Snake Pass before dropping down to the little mill town of Glossop and Chapel-en-le-Frith. The return route is over the limestone plateau of the White Peak and down-dale through Stoney Middleton. Treat the Snake with caution if there is even a hint of snow in the air.

Route Directions

The tour starts in Baslow at the roundabout junction of the A619 and the A623.

1 Head north towards Manchester on the A623 for 2 miles (3.2km) to Calver traffic lights. Turn right on the A625, go ahead on the B6001, signed 'Grindleford', for 2 miles (3.2km) into the town. Here, keep ahead on the B6521 and cross the river bridge up into Nether Padley. Continue for 2 miles (3.2km). Pass Longshaw Lodge, right, and sweep up to a T-junction. Turn left onto the A6187 signed 'Hathersage'. The road bears left and there are fine views of Hathersage Moor. Discarded millstones lie among the birches, near where they were cut – look for one in a car park on the right.

2 Drop down off the moor for 3.5 miles (5.7km) into the village of Hathersage. In the churchyard (on the right up School Lane and Church Bank) is Little John's grave.

3 Drive through Hathersage, then continue along the A6187 for a mile (1.6km) towards Castleton before turning right at traffic lights on to the A6013, signed for Bamford and Ladybower. Continue for 2 miles (3.2km), past the dam wall of Ladybower Reservoir, to a T-junction. Turn left on the A57, signed for Glossop. Continue for another 14 miles (22.5km); going up Woodlands Valley, along Ladybower, then past The Snake Pass Inn. Snake Pass is one of the most exposed and lonely places in England, and the road really does snake its way over the dome of moorland before descending to Glossop.

4 Head into Glossop, turn left at traffic lights onto the A624, signed 'Chapel-en-le-Frith'. Continue for 4 miles (6.4km) to Little Hayfield, then on to Hayfield, with the village on the left and the start of the Sett Valley Trail on the right. Continue ahead for 2 miles (3.2km), past the Lamb Inn. Here there is an imposing sweep of green hills and gritstone walls to the left and a hint of industry, New Mills, and the Derbyshire/Cheshire border away to the right.

5 In a mile (1.6km) the road drops under a railway bridge to a junction. Turn left, signed 'Chapel-en-le-Frith'. Go under two viaducts and a flyover at Chapel Milton and into Chapel-en-le-Frith; go over a roundabout, still signed 'Chapel-en-le-Frith'. Turn left at a junction signed for the A6; turn left, pass beneath the flyover, turn right to join the A6 towards Buxton. Continue for a mile (1.6km), turn left at a roundabout on to the A623, signed 'Chesterfield and Sheffield'. The landscape is different now; limestone country on a gently rolling plateau.

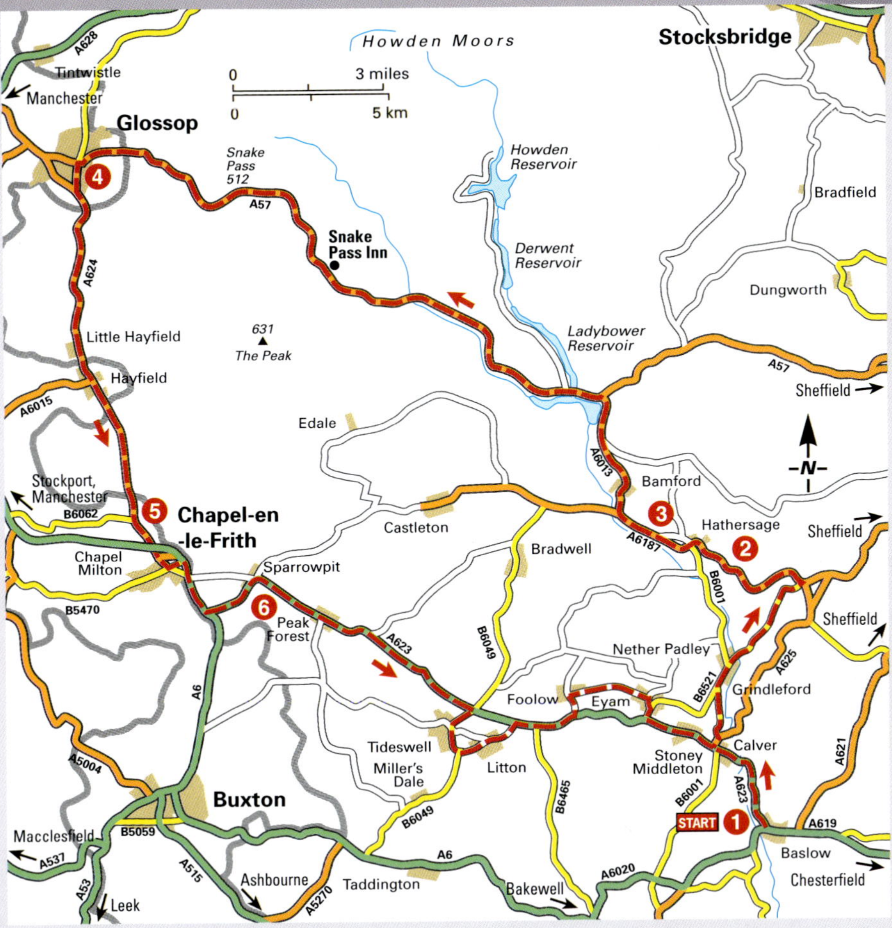

6 After 1.5 miles (2.4km) turn sharp right at The Wanted Inn and continue towards Chesterfield. In 4 miles (6.4km) turn right along the B6049 to Tideswell. Continue beyond the village for 500yds (457m) to a left turn signed (on the right) for Litton. Turn left and drive through this peaceful little village, in 0.75 mile (1.2km) reaching a junction with the A623. Turn right, continue for a mile (1.6km), passing a closed garage and The Three Stags Heads pub. Turn left towards Foolow, then left again to reach the village. Turn right at The Bull's Head Inn and drive the 1.5 miles (2.4km) to Eyam. At the square in the village centre, turn sharp right into The Dale, descending to rejoin the A623; turn left down Middleton Dale into Stoney Middleton. In just 0.75 mile (1.2km), cross over Calver traffic lights, driving 2 miles (3.2km) back to Baslow.

Stanage Edge

A line of dark dramatic cliffs cap the heather moors east of the Derwent Valley. Stanage Edge, the highest of these cliffs, is a great place for walkers to stride out on firm skyline paths with Yorkshire on one side and Derbyshire on the other.

Route Directions

1 At the car park in Hathersage, take the path in the corner past the Methodist church to Main Road. Turn right, cross the road and then turn left in Baulk Lane. The lane climbs steadily north, passing the cricket ground. Beyond the buildings

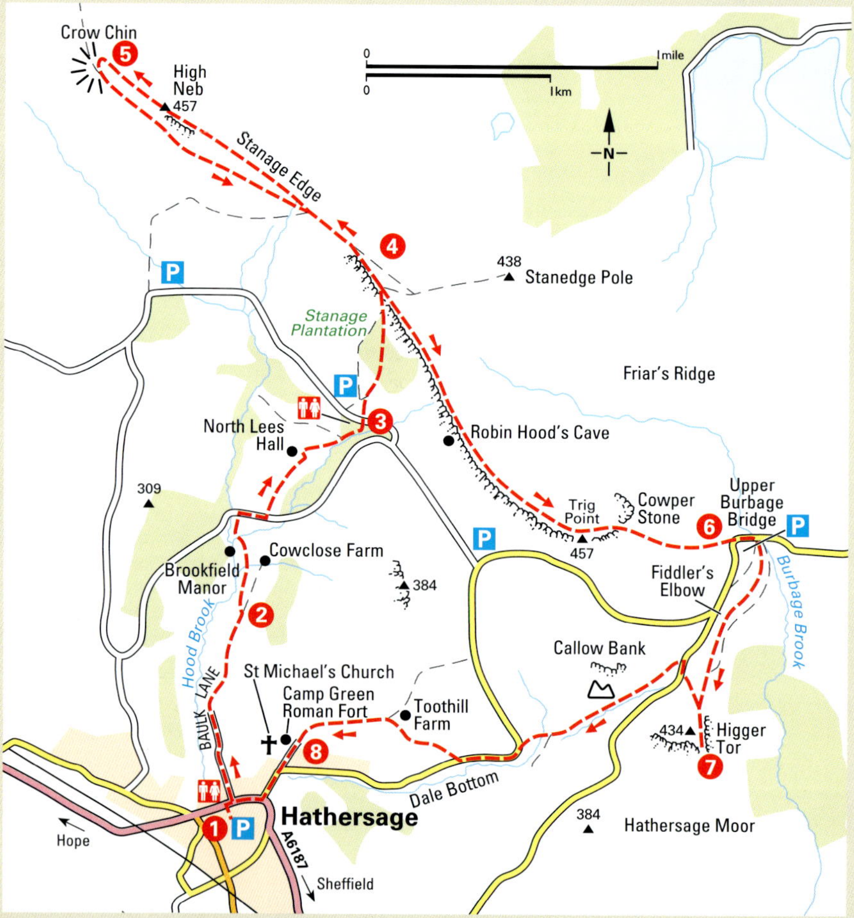

the lane becomes an unsurfaced track.

2 Just short of Cowclose Farm take the signposted left fork, which passes to the right of Brookfield Manor to reach a country lane. Turn right here, then left along a drive to North Lees Hall. After rounding the hall, turn right, climbing some steps that cut the corner to another track. This crosses hillside pastures before continuing through woodland.

3 A stepped path on the left makes a short cut to a roadside toilet block and mountain rescue post. Cross the road for a grassy path heading for the rocks of Stanage Edge. After 200yds (183m) you join the path from the nearby car park. A paved path now climbs through Stanage Plantation before arcing left to the cliff top and turning left.

4 Follow the firm edge-top path north-westwards to see the impressive summit of High Neb and Crow Chin.

5 When you reach Crow Chin, where the edge veers north, descend to a lower path that doubles back beneath the cliffs. This eventually joins a track from the right, which returns the route to the top of the cliffs. Continue walking towards the southeast along the edge to the bouldery east summit (marked on Ordnance Survey maps by a spot height of 457m), whose rocks are capped by a concrete trig point.

6 The track continues to the road at Upper Burbage Bridge. Proceed left along the road for about 150yds (137m), then turn right by the car park, taking the the higher of the two paths which head south to the lofty heights of the summit of Higger Tor.

7 From the rocky top, double back (roughly north of northwest) on a path to the Fiddler's Elbow road. Slightly uphill along the road take the path on the left. This descends Callow Bank to reach a walled track leading down to the Dale Bottom road. Follow the road for 300yds (274m) to a track on the right that traverses the hill slopes to Toothill Farm. Turn left by the farmhouse on a drive that soon joins a tarred lane taking the route down to Hathersage's impressively spired church and the Roman fort of Camp Green.

Route facts

DISTANCE/TIME 9 miles (14.5km) 5h30

MAP OS Explorer OL1 Dark Peak

START Hathersage car park, grid ref SK 232814

TRACKS Well-defined paths and tracks, about 16 stiles and gates

GETTING TO THE START Hathersage is on the A6187 Hope Valley road. From Sheffield take the A625 and turn off right at the signs to Hope, Castleton and various caves. The pay car park in Hathersage is near the swimming pool and is signposted off the main street along Station Road (B6001).

THE PUB The Scotsman's Pack, Hathersage. Tel: 01433 650253

! Do not attempt this walk in misty weather. It is a very long, rewarding walk suitable for experienced family groups.

8 Turn right down School Lane to reach Main Road, which leads you back into the centre of Hathersage. Go left before the toilets to reach the car park at the start of the walk.

The Heights of Abraham

A steady climb raises you above the hurley burley of Matlock Bath to a more familiar Peakland landscape. Above the Heights of Abraham complex, a path leads through woodland. In spring it's heavy with the scent of wild garlic and coloured by a carpet of bluebells. Out of the woods it weaves its way through high pastures, passes through Bonsall and then goes north back into the woods of the Derwent Valley.

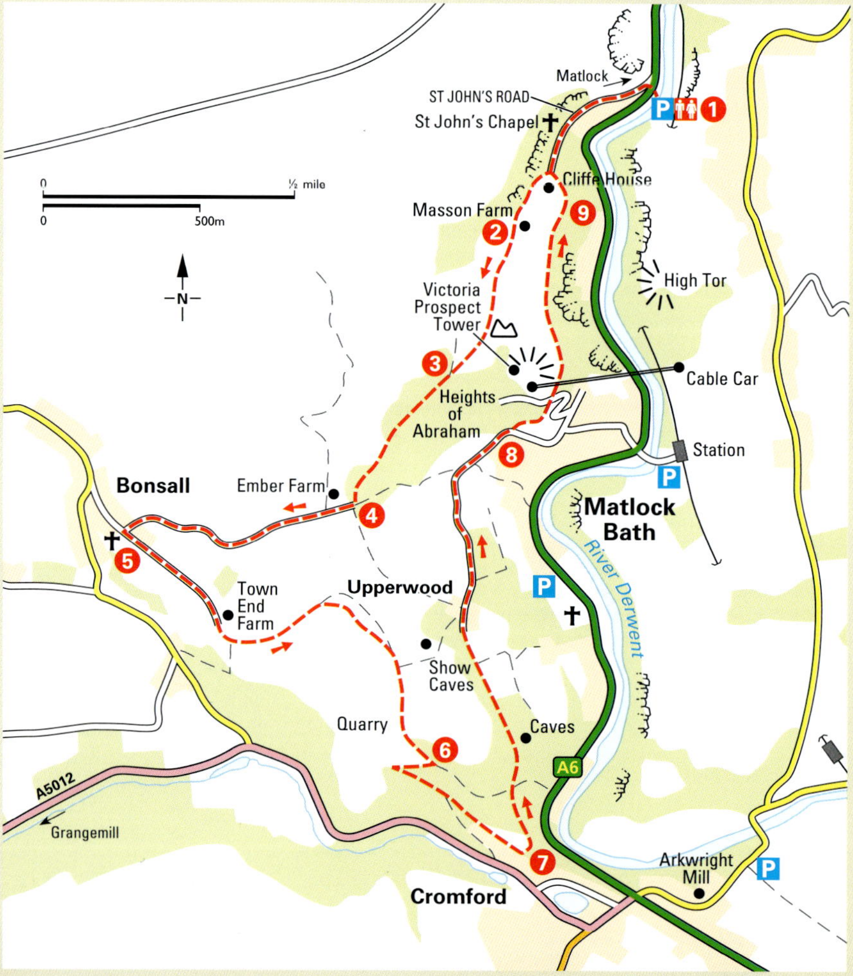

Route Directions

1 Cross the A6 and then take St John's Road up the wooded slopes opposite. It passes beneath St John's Chapel to reach the gates of Cliffe House. Take the path on the right signposted 'Heights of Abraham'. The path climbs steeply upwards through the woods before veering left across the fields above Masson Farm.

2 Beyond the farmhouse and with Victoria Prospect Tower directly ahead, the waymarked path swings right and climbs up to the top of the field. Beyond this the footpath threads through hawthorn thickets before passing one of the entrances to the popular Heights of Abraham complex.

3 Ignore an obvious, engineered path and continue uphill along the perimeter of the complex and then turn left, going over a wall stile. After crossing a wide vehicle track the narrow footpath re-enters woodland.

4 At the far side of the woods, turn right on to a farm track close to Ember Farm. Join a pleasant lane that winds down pastured hill slopes into Bonsall village.

5 Turn left by the church along a lane that becomes unsurfaced when you get beyond Town End Farm. The lane finally comes to an abrupt end by the high fences of a quarry. Turn left here and follow a wide track around the perimeter of the quarry.

6 Where the fence ends, continue down the track, bending sharply right then left along a narrow path through woodland high above the Via Gellia, then take the left fork after about 300yds (274m).

7 Turn left when you reach the next junction, following the footpath waymarked for the Derwent Valley Walk (DVW). This climbs further up the wooded bank, then turns left, tracing a mossy wall on the right. It rakes across the wooded hillside, passes above Cromford Court, then climbs away past some cave entrances to a lane at Upperwood. Ignore the next DVW sign and continue along the lane between cottages and past the West Lodge entrance to the Heights of Abraham showcave.

8 After 100yds (91m) leave the surfaced road for a stepped path, which goes through woods on the left, signed 'Matlock'. Climb some steps to reach a high wooden footbridge over the Heights of Abraham approach road, and then continue on the woodland path. You will pass under the Heights of Abraham cable cars before joining a farm track that comes in from the left.

9 This joins St John's Lane and the outward route at Cliffe House. Retrace your steps to the start.

Route facts

DISTANCE/TIME 8 miles (12.9km) 4h30

MAP OS Explorer OL24 White Peak

START Matlock: pay car park at Artists Corner, grid ref SK 297595

TRACKS Narrow woodland paths, field paths and unsurfaced lanes, several stiles

GETTING TO THE START Matlock Bath is on the A6 between Buxton and Matlock. The car park at Artists Corner is well signed.

THE PUB The King's Head, Bonsall, see Point 4 on route. Tel: 01629 822703

❗ This walk has a long, and in some places, steep opening section before levelling out beside the Heights of Abraham leisure park.

CHESTERFIELD MAP REF SK3871

The tall spire of St Mary's and All Saints Church would have tapered to an elegant pencil-point if its timbers had been properly seasoned. Instead it stands crooked and twisted, a unique landmark, famous for the wrong reasons. Medieval Chesterfield was a prosperous town of guilds; it aspired to have a church that was worthy of its status and was full of fine buildings. Many of these still exist behind shopfronts and occasionally appear when renovation takes place.

Chesterfield is an industrial town. Its heart still beats in time with the coalfields and it is worth visiting for its old inns and good humour. It lies outside the Peak District, but serves its eastern flanks and is a gateway from the M1.

To the north of Chesterfield lies the village of Old Whittington, where a group of daring conspirators led by the Earl of Devonshire met in 1688 to hatch a plot to overthrow the Catholic King James II. The plot was successful; the country welcomed William of Orange and the course of history was changed. The meeting took place in a little thatched inn called the Cock and Pynot, now known as Revolution House and a modest tourist attraction, furnished in 17th-century style and with a video telling the story of the Revolution. Just 2 miles (3.2km) away is Newbold Moor, where the tiny Norman Chapel was attacked in the same year by a mob of Protestants. The chapel, now restored, has a simple weather-beaten charm. Nearby is Tapton House, the home in later life of George Stephenson, the pioneer railway engineer.

CRICH MAP REF SK3454

Perched atop a limestone anticline, the monument on Crich Stand glows from a distance looking like a lighthouse set on alabaster cliffs above a shadowy sea. Three beacon-towers have stood here, but each time they were destroyed by lightning strikes. The present structure dates from 1921 and is a memorial to the men of the Sherwood Foresters Regiment killed in the service of the Crown. The 63-foot (19m) tower is open to the public and offers views across eight counties.

Below the Stand lies a busy working quarry, still eating away at the hill. In its early years George Stephenson built a narrow-gauge railway so that the limestone could be carried to kilns at Ambergate. Now, the worked-out shelf of the quarry is the location of Crich Tramway Village, where more than 40 trams from all over the world are housed. Many are in working order and run every few minutes through a period street, then up onto open countryside. Along the street is the Georgian façade of the Derby Assembly Rooms, relocated here in 1972 after the original building in Derby's Market Place had been badly damaged by fire. Other attractions here are many, and include an enormous exhibition hall and the high-tech sound and vision experience, Tracks in Time.

Crich village is a quiet little place; many of the houses date back to the 18th or early 19th century and were once the homes of stockingers, working on knitting frames by the light of top-storey windows. The Jovial Dutchman pub dates from about the same time.

Visit

A CANAL NATURE RESERVE
Downstream of the Leawood viaduct the Derwent Valley is particularly beautiful; in spring wild daffodils grow on the riverside pastures and the oakwoods ring with the divine sounds of wood warblers, redstarts and pied flycatchers. Located just below Whatstandwell, the overgrown canal is a nature reserve, a haven busy with wildlife; frogs and grass snakes, dragonflies and kingfishers. Take the train to Ambergate and it's possible to walk along the tow path to the next station at Whatstandwell, where there is an excellent pub.

CROMFORD MAP REF SK2956

Road, rail, river and canal run side by side south from Cromford. At first sight it is hard to understand why transport was so important to the place – until 1771 it had been little more than a just a cluster of small cottages around an old packhorse bridge. Until the industrialist Richard Arkwright arrived and set to work to build a cotton mill. Power was plentiful, in the shape of Bonsall Brook and Cromford Moor Sough (the drainage waterway from nearby lead workings) and there was a ready supply of cheap labour due to the decline of the lead-mining industry. Within just a few years Arkwright was rich and the village was a cradle of the Industrial Revolution; three mills were built and lines of gritstone terraced houses accommodated a hardworking workforce who laboured, for long hours, in factories rather than in their own homes. For good and ill the 'Satanic Mills' were the birthplace of the urban working class.

Cromford Canal was built in the early 1790s to link up with the Erewash Canal, which then ran southeast to Nottingham. Cromford Wharf marked its northern terminus, at the mill. A turnpike road was opened up in 1817, then in the 1830s the Cromford and High Peak Railway was constructed, which linked the Cromford Canal with the Peak Forest Canal at Whaley Bridge, thus linking the Trent with the Mersey. In its early years this busy 33-mile (53km) wagonway employed horses on the level stretches and steam winding engines on the inclines. It was considered an extension of the canals and the stations were called wharfs, but by the middle of the 19th century the age of steam had arrived and the Midland Railway was extended north from Ambergate to meet the High Peak line.

Arkwright's Cromford Mill is now undergoing an important restoration programme by the Arkwright Society, who aim to create a lasting monument to his extraordinary genius. There are guided tours, and a visitor centre on the site interprets the mill's heyday. Cromford Canal is popular for family picnics, and there is a tow path walk to High Peak Junction, where there is another visitor centre. The Cromford and High Peak Railway closed in 1967 and is now a popular multi-use recreational trail, the High Peak Trail (the new Pennine Bridleway follows it).

Cromford is made prettier by its large pond, behind the market square, and the Greyhound Hotel (built by Arkwright in 1778). The pond was originally one of the impounding reservoirs to hold water from the Bonsall Brook, but its margins are now the home of ducks and swans. On the other side of the A6, close to the wharf and within sight of Arkwright's elegant homes of Rock House and Willesley Castle, lies the old bridge and its ruined chapel, at the site of the 'crooked ford' that became Cromford.

DARLEY DALE MAP REF SK2663

Four settlements along the Derwent were bound together under the name of Darley Dale a century ago, but the ties were never strong enough to give the place a corporate identity. The A6 has now replaced the railway as the nub of the community, leaving Darley with an artery but no heart.

Darley was the home of Sir Joseph Whitworth, the man who invented the screw thread. Munitions, which included a rifle that fired hexagonal bullets, nuts and bolts, and machine tools soon made him rich, and he bestowed much of his wealth on the local community by not only building a Whitworth Hospital but a Whitworth Hotel, a Whitworth Park and an Institute. Victorian benefactors liked to have their good deeds recognised, but in Whitworth's case his generosity won him few friends and he was not popular. He lived at Stancliffe Hall (not open), guarding his privacy behind high walls and hedges, and when he died in 1887 his dreams of a model village died too.

Beside the A6 lies Stancliffe Quarry. Stone from here was sent to London, where it was used to pave Trafalgar Square and the Embankment. Below this, on the other side of the railway line and on a low mound above the river flats, is Churchtown. Here stands the fine parish church of St Helens, founded by the Normans but rebuilt at the same time as the Old Hall in the 14th century, which once stood a little way further to the north. Most of what is visible on the outside is the result of 19th-century restoration, but there are still plenty of interesting things to see inside; Saxon stones, painted wall designs, the tomb of Sir John de Darley (heart in hands), and the private pew of the reclusive, Sir Joseph Whitworth. The south transept has a stained-glass window by William Morris and Co, produced in the 1860s. The scenes depicted are from the 'Song of Solomon', the chunky figures were by Burne-Jones and the angels probably by William Morris. Victorian stained glass doesn't get any better. (Note that the church is locked when not in use, but the key-holder's telephone number is posted in the porch.)

Above Darley and Northwood lie open fields and woodland before the Derwent meets the Wye at Rowsley. These days the village of Rowsley is most notable as a gateway to the Peak District on the A6, but it used to serve as a railway village with marshalling yards and a large dairy (to supply London with dairy products via the milk train). The main line closed in 1968; it is now home to Peak Rail steam trains. Nearby are the fine Peacock Hotel, a 17th-century manor house, and Caudwell's Mill, an old turbine-driven corn mill. The 19th-century mill is now an interesting craft centre but it still produces flour and visitors can stroll along the paths beside the mill race and alongside the Wye.

THE DERWENT DAMS

MAP REF SK1789

Engineers had their eye on Derwent Dale for decades before work began at Howden Reservoir in 1901. It was the perfect spot; a long deep groove through solid millstone grit, bleak rain-washed moors all around, and only a scattered farming community to relocate. After Howden came Derwent Reservoir, which was completed in 1916. Ladybower, the last and largest, was inaugurated in 1945; as well as flooding 2 miles (3.2km) of the Derwent Valley this also spread up the Woodlands Valley, but not very far because there would be the risk of landslips. Ladybower now holds about 6,000 million gallons of water, the others slightly less; more than a third of the water is piped to Leicester, another third to Sheffield, and the rest is shared between Derby and Nottingham.

Although the sheer scale of the engineering works is impressive, it is the creation of a Canadian-style landscape that draws visitors – big views over great sheets of water, curtains of mist and conifers decked in snow; definitely not very British, but a grand prospect. The forest looks dark and dreary, and there is no doubt that alien conifers are not a substitute for native oak when it comes to bio-diversity. Even so, there are a few surprises. Red squirrels keep a toe-hold here, and in good seed years the local chaffinches are joined by flocks of crossbills. Goshawks are widespread but furtive, except in the early spring when they soar high in display flight over the wooded cloughs.

The Derwent Dams are famous for their drowned villages; when there is a drought thousands of people flock to see a few uncovered stones. The only building to cheat the flood was the Derwent packhorse bridge, dismantled and rebuilt further up the valley to span the river at Slippery Stones. The legendary 617 Dambusters Squadron practised at Derwent Dams before their famous raid on The Ruhr in 1943.

Activity

'TIN TOWN'

Car parks and cycle hire make it easy to explore the western side of the Derwent Valley, along the shores of all three reservoirs and through the forest. By Derwent Reservoir and just south of Birchinlee the road passes beside the site of 'Tin Town', which was once a settlement of corrugated-iron houses provided for the navvies who built the upper reservoirs. For a decade at the beginning of the 20th century it was a self-contained community a thousand strong, with its own school and railway station; all that remains are a few grass-decked foundations and terraces.

GRINDLEFORD MAP REF SK2477

The best way to arrive at Grindleford is by train, either from the east, through the 3.5-mile (5.7km) Totley Tunnel (the second longest in the country) or from the west, back-tracking down the line from Hathersage along one of the prettiest silvan stretches of the Derwent. Before the advent of the Hope Valley line Grindleford was little more than a turnpike crossing (the toll house still stands, next to the bridge), and the nearby settlements of Upper and Nether

Padley were small enough to be lost among the trees. However, the villages bloomed with the opening of the railway station in 1898; most of the houses jostling the slopes and terraces were built by the resulting wave of Sheffield commuters, but not so many houses that the villages merged or lost their backdrop of woodland.

Grindleford Station is actually in Upper Padley. A few hundred yards towards the Derwent, over Burbage Brook and past the converted watermill, lie the ruins of Padley Hall. Very little remains of the 14th-century mansion except foundations. It was once the proud home of the Fitzherbert family, who were Roman Catholics and had the misfortune to be caught harbouring priests at a time when it was illegal to celebrate Mass. In fact the timing could not have been worse; the Spanish Armada had set sail and the country was on the lookout for spies. The two priests, Nicholas Garlick and Robert Ludlam (local men who had been trained in France), were taken to Derby where they were hung, drawn and quartered. John Fitzherbert died in the Tower 30 years later. Padley Hall became the home of one of Elizabeth I's chief priest-catchers before becoming a farm. The gatehouse, which had survived as a barn, was restored in 1933 and is now a chapel; a pilgrimage in memory of the martyrs takes place each July.

In the other direction, following the Burbage Brook upstream, runs a lovely network of paths through Padley Gorge. The boulder-strewn slopes of the gorge are covered in a thick layer of mosses and ferns, thriving in the damp shadows of the ancient oak wood. The trees are sessile oaks rather than pedunculate oaks; the obvious difference is that the sessile acorns are 'sessile' and don't have stalks. Acorns are an autumn bonanza for birds and animals; badgers and squirrels, jays and woodpigeons all make the most of the easy pickings. The spring bonanza is the plentiful crop of caterpillars, gathered from the leaves by migrants, such as pied flycatchers and wood warblers.

Padley Gorge is part of the National Trust's Longshaw Estate. Longshaw Lodge, built as a shooting lodge for the Dukes of Rutland, stands beside the B6521 in attractive grounds. These are now the core of a country park, from where there is access to the moorland above Froggatt Edge. The views all along this most famous Edge are superb, westward over the White Peak and the Dark. To the east rises White Edge on Big Moor, running south to Swine Sty, a Bronze Age settlement in a 'fossilised' landscape of prehistoric fields, picked out among beds of bracken and heather.

HATHERSAGE MAP REF SK2381

Stanage Edge divides featureless moorland from the verdant Derwent. Prehistoric pathways, Roman roads and packhorse trails criss-cross the moors and converge below the confluence of the Derwent and the Noe. On the raised south-facing shoulder of the valley lies Hathersage ('Heather's Edge'), a village built on passing trade and farming. Millstones were a speciality in the 18th century, hewn directly from quarry faces.

Then came the Industrial Revolution and five mills were built, to make pins and needles. The mills had a short life, as did the men who ground the needle-points and had to breathe in the dust.

Whether there ever was a real Little John, or John Nailor, hardly matters. Most visitors want to believe that it really is his grave they see in Hathersage's churchyard. The grave close to the south porch has been excavated several times without producing any bones, though there is a story that a huge thighbone was unearthed here in 1784. In fact the half-hidden stones at the head and foot of the grave were probably set there as the village perch: the standard measure used to mark out acres of land in the days of open-field or strip farming.

The most interesting buildings in Hathersage are along the main road and off School Lane. Past 15th-century Hathersage Hall and Farm, and up the narrow Church Bank, it is possible to walk around Bank Top, a green knoll overlooking the alder-lined Hood Brook and valley. The church crouches on the grassy brow. To the south stands Bell House and The Bell Room, once an inn and barn beside the village green and stocks; to the west stands the Vicarage, and to the east is Camp Green, the ramparts of a 9th-century stockade.

MATLOCK MAP REF SK 2960

Matlock is a tourist honeypot, but there is more to it than the fairy lights and family attractions. Old Matlock stands on the east bank of the Derwent, before it twists west, under the bridge. St Giles Church, the Rectory and Wheatsheaf House mark the original lead-mining settlement at the meeting of packhorse trails and turnpikes. Next door, Matlock Bath is the home of the Peak District Mining Museum, which incorporates Temple Mine, an old lead and restored fluorspar mine, with a self-guided tour that depicts its geology, mineralisation and mining techniques.

Matlock Bath started as a petrifying well and tufa quarry, but in 1696 a bath was cut into the encrusted limestone and a spa was born. In the 18th and early 19th century the cream of society took the waters, staying in fashionable hotels on the sides of the gorge. Then in 1849 the railway arrived and the place was swamped by day trippers.

Matlock Bank, built on the gritstone/shale terraces facing you as you cross the bridge from the south, grew up around a hydropathic spa in the 1850s; the spa was the brainchild of John Smedley, a local mill owner, and it made use of soft water, for bathing in, rather than the thermal spring water available down the road at Matlock Bath. In the early 20th century there were 20 hydros on Matlock Bank and the steep streets had their own tram system.

Today, families come to the Matlocks to visit the popular Gulliver's Kingdom theme park, which is divided into five different worlds each offering many rides and attractions, or to take a cable car up to the Heights of Abraham, with its show caves, nature trail, water gardens and Fossil Factory. Regardless of the other attractions, the cable-car ride is worth taking for the magnificent views down the length of the gorge.

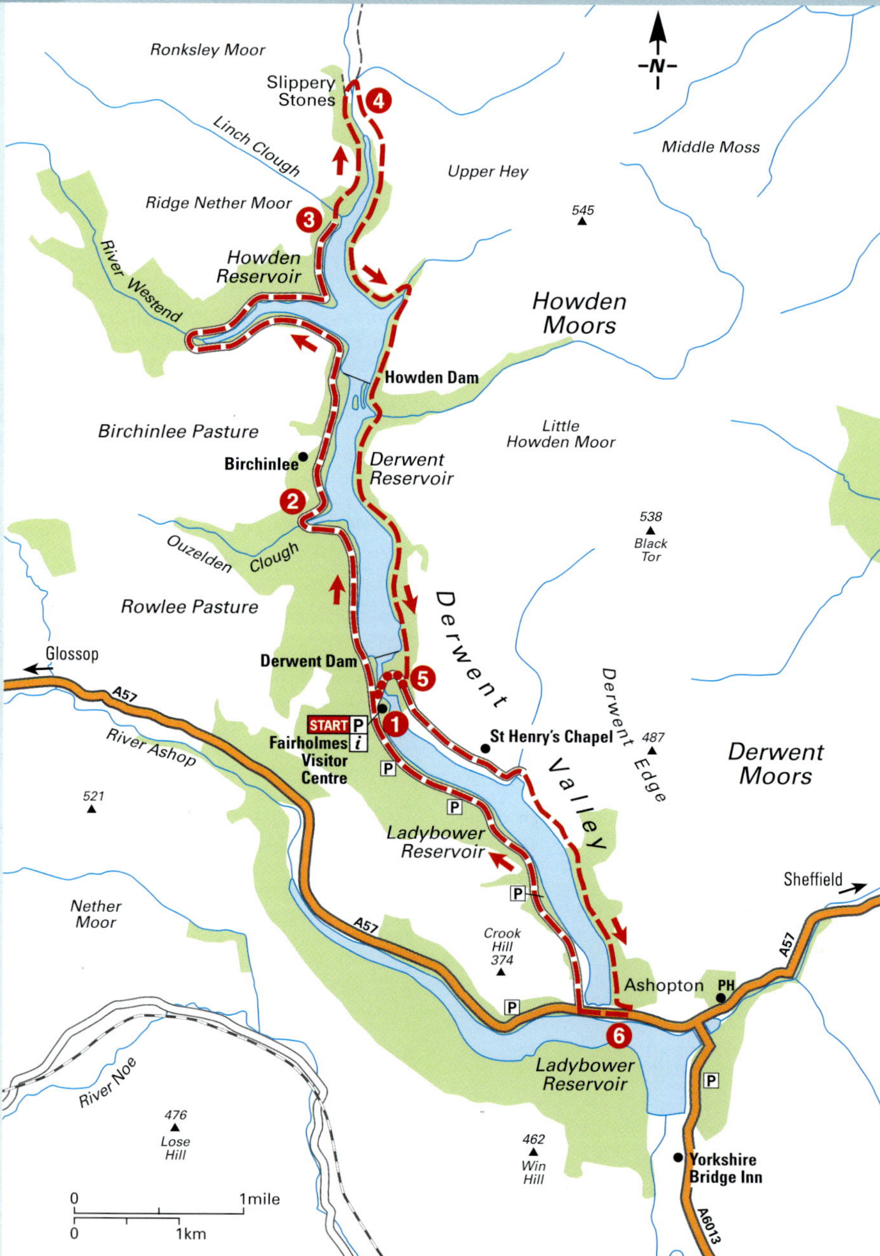
N
Ronksley Moor
Slippery Stones
Linch Clough
Middle Moss
Upper Hey
Ridge Nether Moor
545
River Westend
Howden Reservoir
Howden Moors
Howden Dam
Birchinlee Pasture
Little Howden Moor
Birchinlee
Derwent Reservoir
538
Black Tor
Ouzelden Clough
Rowlee Pasture
Derwent Valley
Glossop
Derwent Dam
Derwent Edge
A57
START
Fairholmes Visitor Centre
St Henry's Chapel
487
River Ashop
Derwent Moors
521
Ladybower Reservoir
Sheffield
Nether Moor
A57
Crook Hill 374
Ashopton
PH
Ladybower Reservoir
River Noe
476
Lose Hill
462
Win Hill
Yorkshire Bridge Inn
A6013
0
1mile
0
1km

The Upper Derwent Valleys

A challenging family route of two halves: a gentle, forested, tarred lane followed by rough upland tracks.

Route Directions

1 Head north from the Fairholmes Visitor Centre, rising to the level of the dam top of Derwent Reservoir. Easy cycling with great views takes you past the memorial to Tip, a sheepdog.

2 Dipping in and out of Ouzelden Clough, the road passes close to the site of Birchinlee, or 'Tin Town'. This village was created to house the workers who constructed the dams. Passing beside Howden Dam, the route now circuits a long arm of Howden Reservoir to arrive at the turning circle at Kings Tree, the end of the tarred road. This is a good place to turn around (9 mile/14.5km round trip) as the next section is more challenging.

3 Beyond the gate the route becomes a rough forest road that climbs gently through the woods above the narrowing tip of Howden Reservoir. At a fork keep right to drop to the old packhorse bridge at Slippery Stones. Just above the bridge swing sharp right to climb the track along the eastern shore of the reservoir.

4 The going is pretty rough for about a mile (1.6km) before a well-graded service road heralds the approach to Howden Dam, particularly colourful in late spring and early summer. A steep, rougher descent follows before the route comes close to the reservoir edge where steep, grassy banks drop straight into the water, so take care here. The track improves considerably as the route nears Derwent Dam. Passing close to one of the towers, the way develops into a tarred lane and passes the first of some isolated houses.

5 You can cut short the ride by turning right to pass the foot of Derwent Dam to return to Fairholmes (9.5 miles/ 15.3km). The main route then continues south passing St Henry's Chapel, becoming rougher again as it rounds an inlet to an interpretation board describing the drowned village of Derwent which stood here until the 1940s.

6 Reaching a gateway, join the tarred lane and drop to the main road. Turn right along the wide cycle path across Ashopton Viaduct, and right again at the far end, following the lane back to Fairholmes Visitor Centre.

Route facts

DISTANCE/TIME 15 miles (24.2km) 4h; shorter alternative route 9 miles (14.5km) 2h30

MAP OS Explorer OL1 Dark Peak

START Fairholmes Visitor Centre, Upper Derwent Valley, grid ref SK 176894

TRACKS Tarred lanes and rough mountain roads

GETTING TO THE START Start at the Fairholmes Visitor Centre in the Upper Derwent Valley. This is signposted off the A57 Glossop to Sheffield road, west of Ashopton Viaduct, which crosses the northern arm of Ladybower Reservoir. Fairholmes is 2 miles (3.2km) along this minor road.

CYCLE HIRE Fairholmes. Tel: 01433 651261

THE PUB The Yorkshire Bridge Inn, Ashopton Road. Tel: 01433 651361; www.yorkshire-bridge.co.uk

! Take care at the start when cycling along a road shared by cars. There are rough tracks on the longer ride. The complete ride is suitable for older family groups using mountain or hybrid-style bikes.

TOURIST INFORMATION CENTRES

Chesterfield
Rykneld Square.
Tel: 01246 345777/8;
www.visitchesterfield.info

Fairholmes
Upper Derwent Visitor Centre.
Tel: 01433 650953;
www.visitpeakdistrict.com

Longshaw Visitor Centre
Tel: 01433 631708

Matlock
Crown Square.
Tel: 01629 583388;
www.visitpeakdistrict.com

PLACES OF INTEREST

Chatsworth House
Tel: 01246 565300;
www.chatsworth.org

Chesterfield Museum and Art Gallery
St Mary's Gate.
Tel: 01245 345727;
www.visitchesterfield.info
Free.

Crich Tramway Village
Crich, Matlock.
Tel: 01773 854321;
www.tramway.co.uk

Cromford Mill
Tel: 01629 823256;
www.arkwrightsociety.org.uk

Heights of Abraham
Matlock Bath.
Tel: 01629 582365; www.heights-of-abraham.co.uk

The Herb Garden
Pilsley. Tel: 01246 854268;
www.theherbgarden.co.uk

High Peak Junction Visitor Centre
Cromford. Tel: 01629 822831

Lea Gardens
3 miles (4.8km) southeast of Matlock, off A6.
Tel: 01629 534380;
www.leagarden.co.uk

Longshaw NT Visitor Centre
Grindleford.
Tel: 01433 637904

Nine Ladies Stone Circle
Stanton Moor. Free.

Peacock Information and Heritage Centre
Low Pavement, Chesterfield.
Tel: 01246 345777
Free.

Peak District Mining Museum
The Pavilion, Matlock Bath.
Tel: 01629 583834;
www.peakmines.co.uk

Peak Rail
Matlock Station, Matlock.
Tel: 01629 580381;
www.peakrail.co.uk

Revolution House
High Street, Old Whittington.
Tel: 01246 345727
Free.

Sir Richard Arkwright's Masson Mills
Matlock Bath.
Tel: 01629 581001;
www.massonmills.co.uk

Whistlestop Countryside Centre
Old Railway Station,
Matlock Bath.
Tel: 01629 580958
Free.

Working Carriage Museum
Red House Stables, Old Road, Darley Dale.
Tel: 01629 733583;
www.workingcarriages.com

FOR CHILDREN

Chatsworth Farm and Adventure Playground
Tel: 01246 565300;
www.chatsworth.org

Gulliver's Kingdom
Temple Walk, Matlock Bath.
Tel: 01629 580540;
www.gulliversfun.co.uk

Matlock Bath Aquarium and Hologram Gallery
110 North Parade.
Tel: 01629 583624; www.matlockbathaquarium.co.uk

Matlock Farm Park
Darley Moor, Matlock.
Tel: 01246 590200
www.matlockfarmpark.co.uk

SHOPPING

Chesterfield
General market, Mon, Fri and Sat; Flea market, Thu.

Matlock
General market, Tue and Fri.

LOCAL SPECIALITIES

Craft Centres
Derbyshire Craft Centre, Calver Bridge.
Tel: 01433 631231
Caudwell's Mill and Craft Centre, Rowsley.
Tel: 01629 733185

Cutlery
David Mellor Cutlery Factory

& Country Shop, The Round Building, Hathersage.
Tel: 01433 650220;
www.davidmellordesign.co.uk

Pottery
Crich Pottery, Market Place, Crich. Tel: 01773 853171

■ PERFORMING ARTS

Pomegranate Theatre
Corporation Street, Chesterfield.
Tel: 01246 345222

The Winding Wheel
Holywell Street, Chesterfield.
Tel: 01246 345334; www.pomegranatetheatre.co.uk

■ SPORTS & ACTIVITIES

ANGLING

Fly
Ladybower Reservoir.
Tel: 01433 651254

CRICKET
Derbyshire County Cricket Ground, Queens Park, Chesterfield.
Tel: 01332 383211

CYCLE HIRE

Bamford
Derwent Cycle Hire, Fairholmes Car Park.
Tel: 01433 651261;
www.peakdistrict.gov.uk

GUIDED WALKS

Derbyshire Dales Countryside Service
Planning and Development Services, Town Hall, Matlock. Full guided walks service.
Tel: 01629 761326

National Park Walks with a Ranger
For more details contact the Peak District National Park Tel: 01629 816200;
www.peakdistrict.org.uk

Peak District
Annual Peak District Walking Festival. Large programme of guided walks held late in late Apr/early May.
Tel: 0870 444 7275; www.visitpeakdistrict.com/walk

HORSE-RIDING

Chesterfield
Alton Riding School.
Tel: 01246 590267

LONG-DISTANCE FOOTPATHS & TRAILS

Derwent Valley Heritage Way
Runs from the Derwent Dams to Derwent Mouth via Derwent Valley Mills World Heritage Site. It is 55 miles (88km) long.

The Limestone Way
A 46-mile (74km) route south from Castleton through White Peak to Rocester (Staffs).

■ ANNUAL EVENTS & CUSTOMS

For the full programme visit www.visitpeakdistrict.com

Bamford
Sheepdog Trials and Country Show, late May.
Well-dressing, mid-Jul.

Chatsworth
Tudor Fair, May.
Horse Trials, mid–late May.
Horticultural Show, late Aug.
Country Fair, early Sep.
Music events, spring–autumn.

Chesterfield
Festive Markets: Easter, Spring Bank Hol, late Jul, late Aug.
Well dressing, early to mid-Sep.

Crich
Transport heritage events throughout the year.

Grindleford
Carnival, mid-Jun.
Padley Pilgrimage, Jul.
Horticultural Show, late Aug (Froggatt).
Sheepdog trials (Longshaw), early Sep.

Hathersage
Well dressing, early Jul.
Horticultural Show, early Sep.

Matlock
Carnival, early to mid-Aug.

Matlock Bath
Illuminations, late Aug–Oct.

Rowsley
Well dressing, late Jun.

Stoney Middleton
Well dressing, with demonstrations, late Jul.

CROMFORD

Tea Rooms

The Grindleford Spring Water Company

Station Approach, Grindleford, Derbyshire S32 2JA. Tel: 01433 631011

Known to generations of walkers and cyclists, this venerable café is tucked next to the west portal of Totley Tunnel, on the Sheffield to Manchester line. Enjoy the full breakfasts, snacks and pint mugs of tea or coffee on offer here.

Post Office Tea Room

Edensor, Derbyshire, DE45 1PH. Tel: 01246 582283

This charming tea room is tucked away just behind the village church and is an integral part of the post office stores, hidden amid the peaceful byroads of the estate village. Expect quality cream teas and dainties, snacks and soups, many made using Chatsworth Estate produce.

The Country Parlour

Caudwell's Mill, Rowsley, Derbyshire DE4 2EB
Tel: 01629 733185

The tea rooms, squeezed between the River Derwent and the mill race, serve scones, cakes and pastries baked on site, many using flour milled next door. Rest easy in old chapel seats and pews, before visiting the craft centre and the mill.

Bookshop Café

Scarthin Books, The Promenade, Cromford, Derbyshire DE4 3QF
Tel: 01629 823272; www.scarthinbooks.com

Books, as well as on-site arts and crafts exhibitions, draw the eye at this quirky little vegetarian café in Cromford. Home-bakes and tea bread, pizzas, Fairtrade coffee, nine kinds of tea and thick soups made from home-grown vegetables are on offer.

Pubs

The Devonshire Arms

Beeley, Derbyshire DE4 2NR
Tel: 01629 733259; www.devonshirebeeley.co.uk

This long-standing pub has everything you'd expect from an old inn – beams, flagstone floors and stone walls. Enjoy the excellent food in the bar, snug or restaurant, with good beers including some brewed on the Chatsworth Estate.

The Chequers Inn

Froggatt Edge, Calver, Derbyshire S32 3ZJ
Tel: 01433 630231; www.chequers-froggatt.com

An old inn with a beer garden on the outside, a chic dining pub within; the best of both worlds is balanced. Expect a smart interior of pastel-yellow walls, polished floorboards and country-cottage furniture. The first-rate menu is to die for, bonuses are the real ales and friendly staff.

Yorkshire Bridge Inn

Ashopton Road, Bamford, Derbyshire S33 0AZ
Tel: 01433 651361; www.yorkshire-bridge.co.uk

This rather lovely rambling place, close to Ladybower Dam, has fires and stoves to rid a winter's chill, and an award-winning flowery beer garden to relax in on summer evenings. The very wide and eclectic menu (including a range of calorific sweets) is supplemented by decent beers.

The Strines Inn

Bradfield Dale, Bradfield, South Yorkshire S6 6JE
Tel: 0114 2851247

This isolated inn is well worth the adventure finding it. Nearly 500 years old, its rooms ooze character, with beams, nooks and crannies sporting all sorts of bric-a-brac. You'll find good, reliable pub grub, a clutch of real ales and a beer garden with excellent views across 'Little Switzerland'.

MAM TOR, CASTLETON

Dark Peak

For six days out of every seven, large cloud banks menace the desolate summits of Bleaklow, Black Hill and Kinder. Snow is almost as likely in June as in January; rain is inevitable. This is high country with a bed of millstone grit lying just beneath the peat; on the surface is a skim of bog moss or cotton grass, and it is the home of curlews and golden plovers. The Pennine Way tracks north along the backbone of England; only two or three roads chance their way across the wilderness here. All of this adds to the attraction, and every now and then there is a sunny day and it is possible to stand on a bank of cloudberry and see for ever.

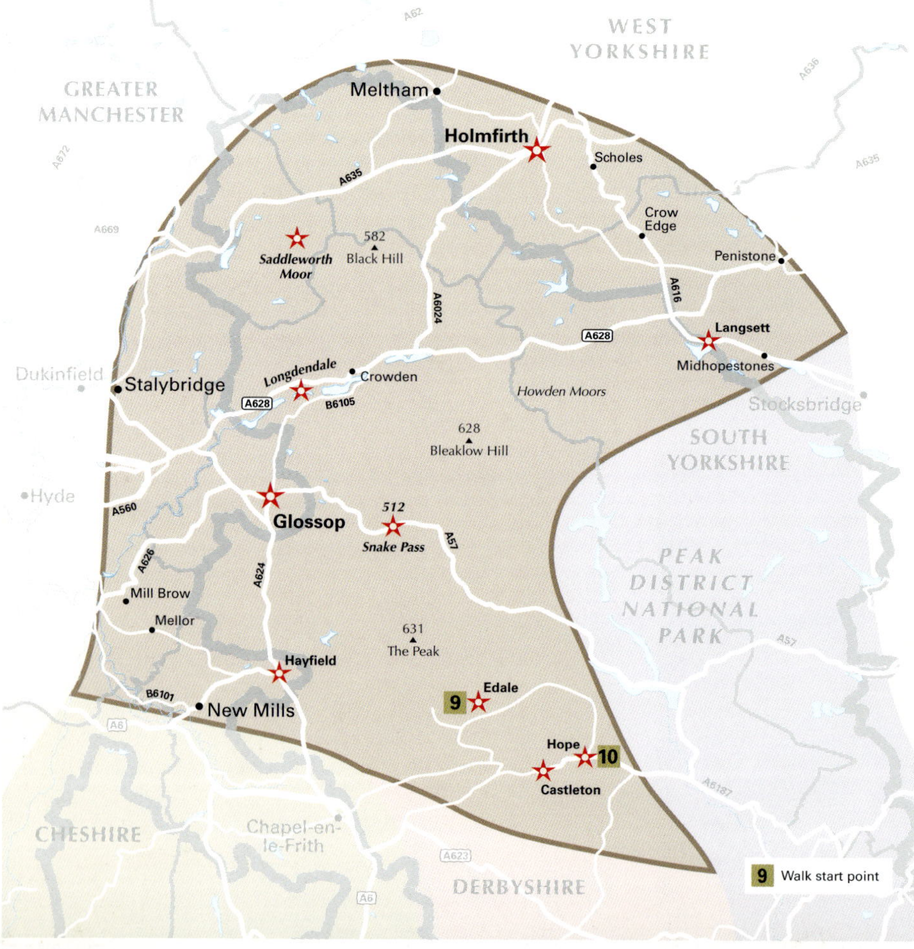

WINNATS PASS, CASTLETON

Unmissable attractions

The Dark Peak lies on a bed of millstone grit beneath peat. The surface is a skin of bog moss or cotton grass, the home of grouse, curlew and plover. Only two or three roads cross this wilderness that, surprisingly, still exists less than a dozen miles from the cities of Manchester and Sheffield. The Pennine Way, Britain's first and toughest long-distance footpath, has its southern terminus at Edale, in the shadow of the Peaks highest hill, Kinder Scout. In the nearby Hope Valley, there is so much of interest that Castleton sometimes suffers from a surfeit of tourists, but it is a good base for exploring the area. Castleton is presided over by the impressively sited ruins of Peveril Castle. Deep beneath the castle is Speedwell Cavern, an old lead mine that descends 2,000 feet (600m). For the more adventurous this part of the Peaks has some of Britain's deepest and most challenging caves.

1 **Edale**
The National Trust owns much of the moorland around Edale. It is busy with visitors in the summer, and over the weekends in winter.

2 **Kinder Scout**
Celebrating the climb to the top of Kinder Scout, and enjoying the reward of far-reaching views, which take in the silvery Kinder Reservoir in the distance.

3 **Blue John Mine**
The mine extends deep into the hillside so, when visiting, remember to wear warm clothes, even on a summer's day, as it will be much colder underground than on the surface.

4 **Edale**
A cyclist tackles the winding Edale road in the Dark Peak. Less arduous routes for cyclists, and walkers, include the Sett Valley Trail which runs from New Mills to Hayfield.

CASTLETON MAP REF SK1582

Castles and caves cast a potent spell; Castleton sometimes suffers from a surfeit of tourists, but there is so much of interest along the upper reach of the Hope Valley that it is impossible not to be drawn into the busy little village, at least as a base from which to wander.

The curtain of high hills at the head of the valley rises to 1,695 feet (517m) at Mam Tor, less than 2 miles (3.2km) to the northwest of the village. Bands of shale and gritstone give the breast-shaped dome of this 'mother-mountain' a terraced appearance; more importantly, the shale is unstable and the whole hillside is gradually slumping down into the valley, taking the old main road with it. In recent years the fate of the road has drawn as many sightseers as the more conventional tourist attractions in the area.

Visit

OAK APPLE DAY

Oak Apple Day, 29 May, is celebrated in Castleton by a glorious pub crawl, involving a procession led by the 'King' and 'Queen', both in Restoration costume and on horseback; the King is completely covered in a great cone of flowers. A silver band plays the traditional tune 'Pudding in a Lantern', girls dance and everyone welcomes the summer. This is Garland day; obscure, colourful and intoxicating. The words of a song capture the spirit of the event:

Thou doesno' know, and I dono' know
What they han i' Brada;
An owd cow's head, and a piece o' bread,
And a pudding baked in a lantern

The tumbled stonework of an Iron Age hill-fort rings the top of Mam Tor; hill-forts were a sign of prestige and status among hostile tribes in those faraway times, and this site must have been the power-base of an important chieftain. When the Romans arrived the local community had to learn a new way of life; from 'Celtic cowboys' of the open hills they became hewers and delvers in the dusty darkness of the lead mines.

Mining, for galena or lead ore, was a major industry in the Castleton area for the best part of 2,000 years, and it has left its scars. Grassy mounds and tree-lined ditches hide old spoil-heaps and rakes or veins. Many of the spoil-heaps were reworked for other minerals, such as fluorspar and blende, and natural limestone caves were enlarged. Despite the fact that the Derbyshire mines yield no silver, the area west of Castleton, up the winding road to Winnats Pass, is famous for its Blue John, a deep purple form of fluorspar.

The Treak Cliff, Speedwell, Peak Cavern and Blue John Mine 'show caves' are open to the public. Of these, Treak Cliff is an old lead mine, rich in veins of the mineral known as Blue John and is still worked, while the Speedwell Mine is special because the main workings (and the 'Bottomless Pit') can only be approached by boat, floating along an along an underground 'canal' or flooded tunnel. Peak Cavern, close to Castleton, is set into Castle Hill on the south side of the valley and has a natural entrance – 100 feet (30.5m) across and 50 feet (15.2m) high. All the caves are exciting to explore, even as part of a guided tour.

Castleton owes its name and very existence to Peveril Castle, perched on Castle Hill. Peveril was built by William de Peverel, a favourite of William the Conqueror, in 1076. All mineral rights belonged to the king, who therefore had good reason to set a friend up with an overview of the lucrative lead-mining area. The castle also happened to be in the heart of the Peak Forest, prime hunting country; Normans liked to mix profit with pleasure.

Peveril Castle is managed by English Heritage and is open to the public. The footpath up to it is steep and sometimes slippery, but the views from the curtain wall are exceptionally good. Cave Dale, a sheer-sided limestone gorge, forms a natural defence to the south and east; to the west is Peak Cavern and to the north is Hope Valley and the gritstone hills.

EDALE MAP REF SK1285

Edale is the name given to the upper reaches of the River Noe as it threads its way through a broad valley of pastures and meadowlands. Five ancient farming communities, the Booths, are scattered along the north slope of the valley, tucked in beneath the desolation of the Kinder plateau but above the wilderness of the river. 'Booths' were barns or cowsheds, refuges for stock and farming families in troubled times; they have grown into hamlets and villages linked by green meadows and twisting lanes.

Grindsbrook Booth lies at the heart of the dale and can be anything but calm on sunny Sundays. Edale is the threshold of the high hills, the access point to Kinder. It marks the start of the Pennine Way, the first long-distance footpath in Britain, and is a magnet for walkers. Sitting outside the Old Nag's Head Inn and watching a constant tide of seriously keen walkers disappearing up the track can be a little daunting; in fact most visitors to Kinder are only there for the day and only go a few miles. For those intending to walk the whole 256 miles (412km) of the Pennine Way, the really testing ground is the high Kinder and Bleaklow plateau, a wilderness of sodden peat. But there is good walking on a track before that, from opposite the Old Nag's Head, along a footpath signed Hayfield and westwards along the old packhorse trail.

This route, now well-established as the official start of the Pennine Way, takes you through Upper Booth and up Jacob's Ladder, a set of zig-zag steps cut into the hillside. Edale Cross marks the meeting of the three wards of the Royal Forest of the Peak, and then it is only a few hundred yards north to Kinder Low and Kinder Downfall, the waterfall that sometimes gets blown uphill in the teeth of the western gales. A stiff walk, but worthwhile for the views to the west are very special.

Visit

'WHETHER THE WEATHER BE WET'
Edale is not a place to linger in the rain; 60 inches (152cm) a year fall on Kinder, and the Booths get their share. Nor is there very much cover. On crisp winter mornings it can be cold in the valley, as frost rolls down from the summits, but this is certainly the time to appreciate the elemental landscape and the far horizons.

GLOSSOP MAP REF SK0393

Textiles breathed life into Glossop; there was water power and coal a-plenty and a workforce who came from Stockport and Manchester. At the turn of the 19th century there were more than 56 mills in the eight townships of Glossopdale; most were cotton mills, but there were also paper mills, ropewalks and woollen mills. Not many thrived; those that did modernised with the times and took to power looms, which were steam-driven and needed more water and more coal.

The settlement expanded in the early 19th century under the patronage of the Duke of Norfolk and at one time it was named Howard Town (Howard is the family name of the Duke), to distinguish it from Old Glossop, the village uphill to the east. The name Glossop came from Glott Hop, 'hop' being a valley and 'glott' a much earlier lord of the manor. But it was the Howards who left the greatest mark on the new community and who were responsible for most of the town's important buildings, such as the Market Hall and the Railway Station. The heart of Glossop is Norfolk Square, which still has a prim elegance and is surrounded by interesting shops, including a small heritage centre.

Glossop suffered disastrously when the cotton industry collapsed in the 1920s, and it took decades to recover. Overspill housing from the 1960s has affected the character of the town too, but there are some fascinating nooks and crannies, hidden away in the fabric of the place. Just beyond the housing estate of Gamesley lies the remains of the Agricolan Roman fort of Melandra Castle, while to the north of the town, near Howard Park, is Mouselow or Castle Hill, with important Bronze Age and Iron Age associations and the site of a motte and bailey built by William de Peverel. Glossop's roads to the east lead to Longdendale and the Snake Pass, while only a few miles to the west is the M67 and Manchester.

HAYFIELD MAP REF SK0386

The picturesque name and rural setting disguise Hayfield's industrial past; the village once hummed and rattled to the sound of cotton and paper mills, calico printing and dye works. It has also resounded to marching feet and cries of protest – in 1830 a mob of 1,000 mill workers gathered to demand a living wage and were dispersed by hussars. Eleven men appeared at Derby Assizes as a result, but the cotton industry was in terminal decline and all the anger was in vain. A century later, on 24 April 1932, Hayfield was the starting point for the 'mass trespass' of ramblers onto Kinder Scout. This protest eventually resulted in 'the right to roam'.

Hayfield is a peaceful little village, catering for tourists of all kinds. It has plenty of little cafés and restaurants with quaint and inventive names. One of the most revealing places to while away a few minutes is by the bridge, next to the courtyard of the Royal Hotel, which looks out over the River Sett, from the war memorial to the jumble of cottages and sloping roofs at the back of Church Street. Nearby is St Matthew's Church, built on the foundations of an older church washed away in a flood.

Serious walkers head east out of the village, up and over the green foothills to the russet expanse of the Kinder plateau. Families and other easy-going ramblers head west along the Sett Valley Trail towards New Mills. The car park at the start of this 3-mile (4.8km) trail, separated from the main village by the A624, was once the railway station, and the trail follows the course of the single-track line. In its heyday thousands of visitors arrived here from Manchester via the New Mills branch line; Hayfield marked the end of the mill towns and the start of the countryside.

HOLMFIRTH MAP REF SE1408

Before the BBC television series *Last of the Summer Wine* became a national institution, the most famous comic characters to come out of Holmfirth were depicted on postcards published by Bamforths. Saucy seaside cartoons became a serious business for the family firm just after World War I; they had already pioneered lantern slides and the motion picture industry but were outflanked in the end by Hollywood.

The town of Holmfirth is a gem, built at the confluence of the Holme and the Ribble, where the Norman Earl Warren built a corn mill. For several centuries the lower valley was left to the wild wood and the hilltop towns of Cartworth, Upperthong and Wooldale prospered, combining farming with weaving. There are fine stone farmhouses and cottages on the upper slopes of the valley, often absorbed into the outskirts of the newer town, to tell the tale of prosperity. With the expansion of the cotton mills in the mid-19th century tiers of three-storey terraced cottages sprang up lower and lower into the valley and eventually cotton mills crowded the riverside. The fast-flowing river was harnessed but never tamed; it still floods when the Pennine snows melt too quickly.

Holmfirth has to be explored at a gentle pace, because most of the streets are steep. From Victoria Bridge in the middle of the town it is possible to wander up Penny Lane, round the back of the church where the surrounding hills peep out between chimney pots and sooty walls, and down cobbled lanes worn shiny and smooth by a million clogs. Somewhere along the way you can be almost certain to arrive at Sid's Café, or The Wrinkled Stocking Café, next door to Nora Batty's on the river.

Insight

THE PENNINE WAY

When it is spring in the valley and there are daffodils all over Holmfirth it is sobering to look to the west and see the clouds still gathered over Wessenden and Saddleworth Moors, and the snow lying on the summit of Black Hill. It looks a frightening prospect, but thousands of walkers tackle it each year as part of the Pennine Way National Trail. The Pennine Way has existed for more than 40 years, and in that time places like Featherbed Moss and Wessenden Head have gained notoriety, quite deserved, for their evil bogs. These days most of the worst bits are stone-flagged to create causey paths like the old packhorse trails. Even so, the Pennine Way is a challenge, and the pubs and guesthouses of Holmfirth are a welcome diversion.

Pennine Ways on Kinder Scout

One end of the Pennine long-distance trail ascends to the craggy outcrops of the Kinder plateau. An edge walk goes round the great chasm of Grindsbrook and passes the gritstone sculptures of Grindslow Knoll to the ravine of Crowden Brook. The route descends by the brook passing waterfalls then crosses the fields of Edale.

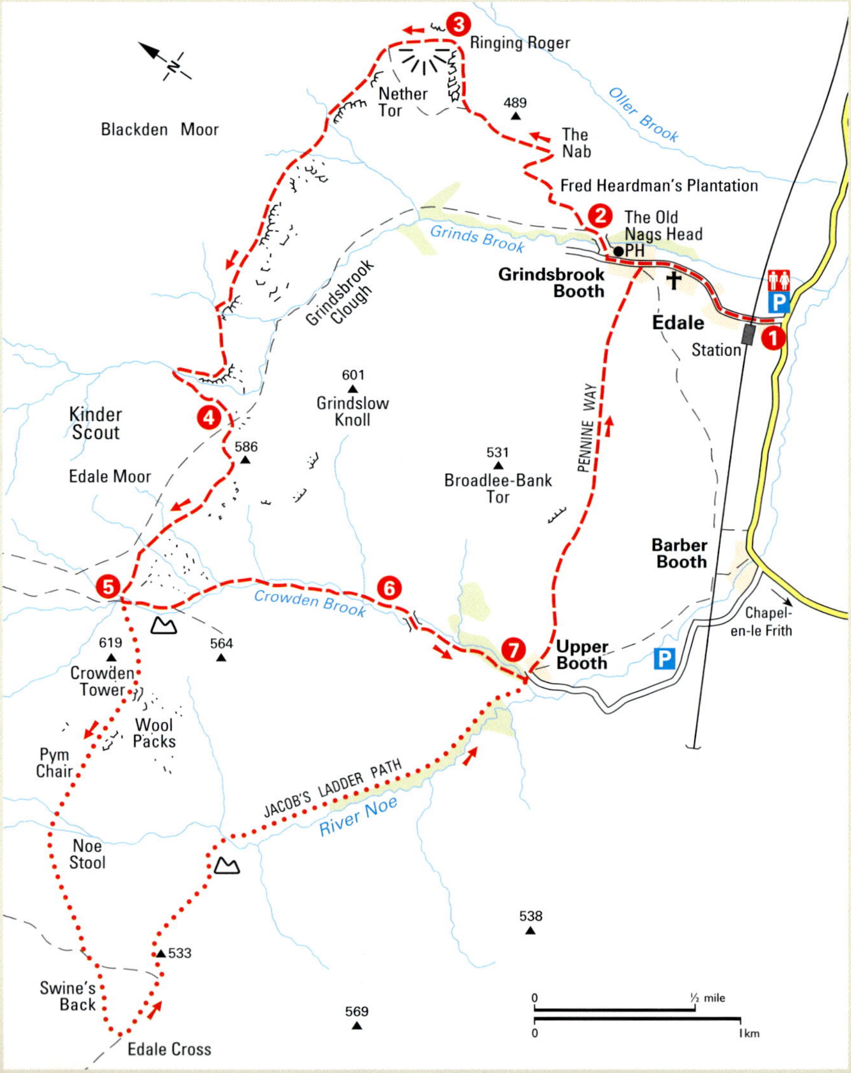

Route Directions

1 Turn right out of the car park and head north along the lane into Edale village, under the railway and past The Old Nags Head. At the end, turn right and follow the path across the footbridge over Grinds Brook.

2 Leave the main Grindsbrook Clough path by the side of a barn, taking the right fork that climbs up the lower hillslope to a stile on the edge of open country. Beyond the stile the path zig-zags above Fred Heardman's Plantation then climbs up the nose of The Nab to the skyline rocks. Where the path divides, take the right fork to the summit of Ringing Roger.

3 Follow the edge path left, rounding the cavernous hollow of Grindsbrook past Nether Tor. The old Pennine Way route is met on the east side by a large cairn.

4 Ignoring the left fork heading for the outlier of Grindslow Knoll, follow the paved footpath westwards to reach the head of another deep hollow, the clough of Crowden Brook.

5 Cross over Crowden Brook, and then immediately leave the edge to follow a narrow level path traversing slopes on the left beneath the imposing outcrop of Crowden Tower. Below the tower, fork left for a steep and, at first, rough track down to the banks of the brook. The path now follows the brook, fording the path on several occasions.

6 Cross a stile at the edge of open country and then go across a footbridge shaded by tall rowans to change to the west bank. From here the path threads through woodland before descending in steps to the road at Upper Booth. You now need to follow the Pennine Way path back to Edale.

7 Turn left along the road and then left again into the farmyard of Upper Booth Farm before exiting at the top right corner. After following a track to a gateway, bear left uphill to a stile by an old barn. Here the Way traverses fields at the foot of Broadlee Bank before joining a tree-lined track into the village. Turn right along the road back to the car park.

Extending the Walk

You can extend this walk from Point **5**, continuing along the edge of the Kinder plateau, then descending to Upper Booth on the Pennine Way route by Jacob's Ladder to then rejoin the main walk at Point **7**.

Route facts

DISTANCE/TIME 5 miles (8km) 3h30

MAP OS Explorer OL1 Dark Peak

START Edale pay car park; grid ref SK 125853

TRACKS Rock and peat paths, about 16 stiles and gates

GETTING TO THE START From Sheffield take the A625 and follow the brown tourist signs for the caverns at Castleton. At Hope, turn right for Edale opposite the church; in 5 miles (8km) turn right into Edale's car park. Edale Station is served by trains on the Sheffield to Manchester line.

THE PUB The Old Nags Head, Hope Valley. Tel: 01433 670291

! There is a long, steep climb near the start of this walk. The return route from Crowden Tower is very steep and can be slippery. This walks is recommended for experienced family walking groups only.

Over Win Hill

This walk from Castleton to Win Hill threads through pastures above the River Noe. In one of the riverside fields the path comes across the earthwork remains of the Roman fort, Navio, built in the time of Emperor Antoninus Pius. At its peak it would have sheltered 500 soldiers. Win Hill looms ahead as you cross the valley and climb towards it. Pass through the hamlet of Aston then continue the climb up a stony track through bracken and grass to the summit of Win Hill and a concrete trig point. Below, the view takes in Ladybower Reservoir, while the gritstone tors of Kinder Scout, the Derwent Edge, and Bleaklow fill the northern horizon.

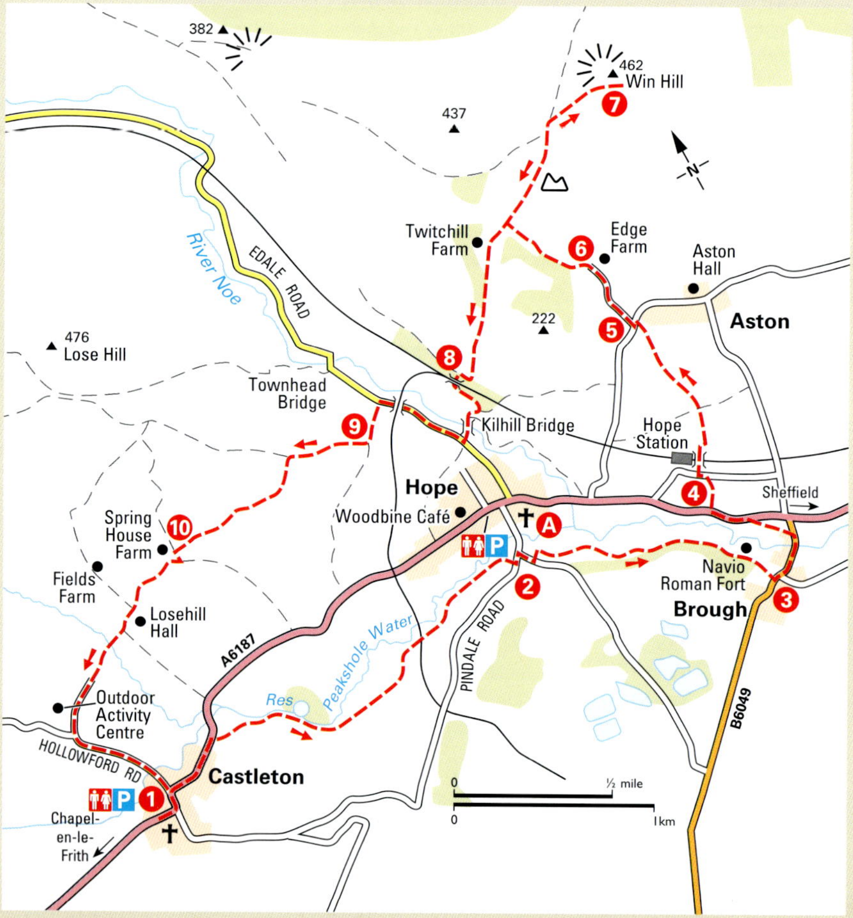

Route Directions

1 Turn left out of the car park along the main street. At the far end of the village turn right on a walled stony lane and continue along a well-defined path accompanying Peakshole Water. Cross the railway with care and continue along the path to its end at Pindale Road.

2 Turn left here, then right at the next junction. After 200yds (183m), go over a stile by a gate on the left and follow the path running roughly parallel to the lane at first, then the River Noe, to reach the site of the Roman fort of Navio. Beyond the earthworks go over a stile in a fence and bear half right across another field to reach the B6049 road at Brough.

3 Turn left through the village and cross the footbridge over the River Noe. Go left over a stile and head northwest to the A6187. Cross over and turn left along the road for 200yds (183m) to a small gate just beyond a cottage. Follow the hedge and dyke on the right to pass to the right of some houses.

4 Turn left along the lane heading towards the railway station, then go right along a narrow path, which leads to a footbridge over the line. Cross the bridge and turn right at its far end, then left through a gate to cross yet more fields, this time keeping the fence on your right.

5 When you reach Aston turn left along the road, then almost immediately turn right along a narrow, surfaced lane, signposted 'Win Hill and Hope Cross'.

6 Beyond Edge Farm an unsurfaced track on the left takes the route along the top edge of some woods to a path junction above Twitchill Farm. Now climb right on a well-used path to Win Hill's summit.

7 From the summit retrace your steps back to the junction above Twitchill Farm. This time descend left past the farm on the surfaced drive to the railway.

8 Turn left under the railway tunnel for the lane via Kilhill Bridge to Edale Road. Turn right along the road, under the railway bridge, then turn left by a red postbox in a wall on a field path.

9 By the outbuildings of a cottage, turn right on a path climbing towards Lose Hill. Take the left fork at a junction of paths to follow a waymarked route signposted to Castleton westwards to Spring House Farm.

10 In front of the farm, turn right to walk along a track behind Losehill Hall. Where the lane swings left, leave it to follow a cross-field path, which joins a rough lane. After passing the outdoor centre, turn left along Hollowford Road into Castleton.

Route facts

DISTANCE/TIME 8.75 miles (14.1km) 5h

MAP OS Explorer OL1 Dark Peak; grid ref SK 149829

START Castleton pay car park

TRACKS Paths can be slippery after rain, several stiles

GETTING TO THE START From Sheffield take the A625 southwest and turn on to the A6187 near Hathersage, following the brown tourist signs for the Caverns at Castleton. The car park is in the centre of Castleton.

THE PUB The Cheshire Cheese Inn, Edale Road, Hope. Tel: 01433 620381

❶ The short scramble up to the summit of Win Hill is steep. Take care crossing the main road near Brough.

HOPE VALLEY

HOPE MAP REF SK1783

The Hope Valley is the main access route from the Derwent Valley through to Castleton, Edale and the Dark Peak, so the road is often busy. The little village of Hope lies at the confluence of the Noe and the Peakshole Water, which emerges from the bowels of the earth 2 miles (3.2km) away at Castleton. Hope railway station lies half a mile (800m) out of the village, across the Noe to the east, and is a perfect starting point for a walk up Win Hill, one of the best bracing viewpoints in the whole Peak. Lose Hill, the dark twin of Win Hill and another fine viewpoint, lies due west on the opposite side of the Noe.

Hope Church is in the heart of the village and is a typically solid, squat-spired affair, which dates back to the 14th century. Inside there are two stone coffin lids bearing hunting horns, the motif of royal forest huntsmen. Outside, next to the porch, is the shaft of a Saxon cross with vague weathered carvings on its face. Stone scrollwork on preaching crosses represents the height of Dark Age culture and the Peak District has some fine examples.

South of Hope stands the Blue Circle cement works, undeniably a blot on the skyline and difficult to reconcile with a National Park except as a source of local employment (but perhaps tourists of the future will come specially to see it, just as today's visitors explore old lead workings and derelict mills). Other landscape features are dwarfed in the presence of this monolith, but it marks the dividing line between the gritstone and limestone; the fields to the south are bright green and enclosed in an intricate mesh of grey drystone walls.

The village of Bradwell lies only a couple of miles from Hope but it is completely different in character, full of steep twisty lanes and lead-miners' cottages. A ridge called the Grey Ditch climbs the slope to Rebellion Knoll and may be a trace of the boundary between the Dark Age kingdoms of Mercia and Northumbria. Nearby, accessible by a riverside path from Hope, lies the site of a Roman fort. There is little to see on the ground, the stonework having been plundered long ago to build local farmhouses and Hope church.

LANGSETT MAP REF SE2100

The northeast corner of the Peaks is probably the least visited sweep of country for 50 miles (80.5km) around; driving south from Holmfirth or west from Penistone takes you across open moors and plateaux with the whole of Yorkshire spread out below in a cerulean haze. There are very few villages to catch your immediate attention, but the upper valleys of the Don and the Porter, which rise on the same watershed as the Derwent on Howden Moor, are full of interest. The Porter has been dammed in several places above Stocksbridge and there are good access points to the reservoirs and riverside and high up onto the moors.

Langsett provides the best starting point for an exploration of the Porter and its string of pearls. Before Sheffield Corporation bought up the valley for water catchment this area was farmland, with some of the finest

Visit

WHAT IS A NATIONAL PARK?
Britain's National Parks are not national property. Most of the land is still privately owned, but the area is administered by a National Park Authority. It is their task to strike an appropriate – and often fragile – balance between the conservation of the park's landscape, architecture and wildlife, while still ensuring that the local people and landowners can make a living and that the millions of visitors and walkers have access to use and appreciate the park's landscape. The National Park Authority in the Peak District operates a number of Information Centres, such as the one at Langsett, which provides a wide range of information, publications and organises walks and talks in and about the area.

medieval cruck-framed farmhouses and barns in the country. Many of the buildings survive today, some still as dwellings but few as working farms.

Langsett Barn bears a datestone of 1621 and is now the village hall but it is open during the season as a National Park Information Centre, and is worth a visit both for information and displays about the park and to see the solid functional beauty of the barn's ancient post and truss construction.

Heading out from the car park it is possible to explore the woodlands and shoreline of Langsett Reservoir or walk along the dam wall, past the crenellated valve tower (a miniature of a tower at Lancaster Castle), to the old stone-built hamlet of Upper Midhope.

Above Langsett Reservoir, the Brook House Bridge gives access to the ancient trackway of the Cut Gate, an old drovers' road which started at Derwent and leads all the way to Penistone. The track climbs south over Midhope Moor, which is uncompromising high ground inhabited mostly by mountain hares and short-eared owls, littered with ancient flints and overlooked by the burial mound of Pike Lowe. This is not a good place to get caught in bad weather.

LONGDENDALE MAP REF SK0397

Above Glossop a cleft in the most desolate wilderness of Peak moorland runs north by northeast from the little town of Tintwistle to the Derbyshire-Yorkshire border, shielding the A628 as it climbs to Gallows Moss. Down the cleft runs the River Etherow, a tributary of the Mersey. Over a century ago the valley was dammed to create five reservoirs, and this has so altered the character of the place that it sometimes looks like an oasis in a desert; green woodland and pasture encircles pools of silver, over which white sailing dinghies pirouette and scud.

Longdendale is a favourite place for day trips out of Manchester, and the cultural roots of Tintwistle are entwined with the old Lancashire cotton mills. The waters of the Etherow were harnessed to power the mills and were dammed to provide water for the city. A wealth of railway lines were laid to link the great industrial cities of Manchester and Sheffield, following the valley up to Woodhead and the Prough, a 3-mile (4.8km) tunnel below the moors. But now all that is in the distant past; the weavers' cottages of Tintwistle are now picturesque and the course of the railway is a footpath. Nevertheless, the dale still serves the city in its own way and remains part of its heritage.

The graveyard of lonely Woodhead Chapel, set on a shoulder above the banks of the upper reservoir, contains the last resting place of navvies and their families who died of cholera while the second railway tunnel was being built in 1849. Crowden, above Torside Reservoir, is a famous youth hostel on the route of the Pennine Way and is a welcome sight to walkers after the rigours of Bleaklow to the south or Black Hill to the north. Apart from a few isolated farms and an Information Centre there are no other settlements in the valley; despite the fine scenery Longdendale often suffers from a wild climate, in the shadow of the moors.

SADDLEWORTH MAP REF SD9906

The gorge of the river Tame forms the boundary of the National Park in the northwest. Slicing between Saddleworth Moor and the West Pennines, this defile hosts a string of picturesque gritstone villages that breathe Yorkshire charm and character into an area with a history stretching back to the Romans (the site of a fortlet stands beside the remote reservoirs at Castleshaw). Saddleworth itself is a nebulous area; there's no village of that name here – the great sweep of moors arcing west from Holmfirth and the villages take that collective name, an area that was part of Yorkshire's West Riding until 1974 and decidedly proud of this fact. The largest village is Uppermill, strung alongside the Huddersfield Narrow Canal and crammed with craft and antique shops, restaurants and inns; the Saddleworth Museum offers a succinct overview of the area. Just to the north, locks rise to Britain's longest canal tunnel at Standedge, over 3 miles (4.8km) long.

The most charismatic village is Dobcross, huddled around a tiny cobbled square stapled to the end of Harrop Edge, from which narrow lanes and ginnels lined with three-storey weaver's cottages plummet to old mills in the valley bottom. Film buffs may recognise the square from the 1979 film *Yanks*. Further up the Tame, Delph retains perhaps the most 'industrial' feel of all the villages, its mills gradually morphing into trendy apartments below bluffs and crags smothered by bilberry and heather.

Linking these and the other villages of Saddleworth is the remarkable Longwood Thump Rushcart Festival. Held over the second weekend after the 12 August, this celebration centres on a cart, pulled by teams of men, that is decorated by a high pyramid of rushes, atop which a hapless soul must sit in a chair while touring the churches and inns of the area. The phrase 'Going on the Wagon' is said to originate here.

A visit to the Church Inn, high above Uppermill, where the festival is based, will reveal much. In the graveyard next door is a fascinating memorial to victims of a double murder – the 'Bill o' Jacks murders', unsolved since 1832. Myriad footpaths string southwards to some fine, challenging walks around and above Dovestone Reservoir, set in a landscape of cloughs, moors, edges and wind-sculpted pinnacles.

THE SNAKE PASS

MAP REF SK 0892

Weather warnings on television and radio have made The Snake Pass famous; when the sun is shining across the rest of the Pennines, The Snake Pass, the A57 between Sheffield and Manchester, may be closed because of severe blizzards.

The road from Ladybower and the Woodlands Valley strikes northwest, sheltered on a shoulder of the River Ashop, but after Lady Clough it has nowhere to hide and crosses a windswept desert at 1,680 feet (512m). Bleaklow lies to the north, Kinder Scout to the south. In places the peat has been stripped away to reveal a surface of shattered stones, which is how the glaciers left the place after the Ice Age. There are no trees, no barns or walls. Not a good place to be stuck in a car.

Of course, the remote wildness of The Snake is irresistible and in fine weather, with the sun shining on the heather, it can be magical. The upper Woodlands Valley is pretty, dotted with old farms and birch-lined cloughs. Most of the Peak District has been designated as an Environmentally Sensitive Area, which means that farmers get special payments for agreeing to manage the land with conservation as a priority. In the case of the high moors, the most important thing is the stocking rate – fewer sheep are now overwintered on the heather, and this should benefit the flora and fauna.

A tributary of the Ashop runs north to Alport Dale and Alport Castle, which is not a castle at all, but an outcrop of rock; this is accessible by a bridleway and makes a good walk. The barn of Alport Castle Farm is used on the first Sunday in July each year for a Lovefeast service. These 'love feasts' originated during the 18th-century religious revival that was spearheaded by the Wesley brothers. They converted multitudes of workers, from mines and mills, farms and factories, to a pattern of religious life which inspired them to build a number of 'wayside Bethels' in remote places. Along with field preaching, their ministers organised camp meetings and covenant services, incorporating 'love feasts', which were based on the meetings of the early Church.

Back along the Snake Road there are two or three last farms and cottages before you reach the lonely Snake Pass Inn. At the top of Lady Clough, on the highest and most featureless ground, The Snake is crossed by the Pennine Way, close to the paved trackway of ancient Doctor's Gate. Travellers have been venturing across these moors for thousands of years, often with a shiver of apprehension.

Visit

THE SNAKE PASS INN

The Snake Inn was built in 1821 as Lady Clough House, when the original medieval track was transformed into a turnpike road. If any visitor should need a reminder about how remote this hostelry is, there is a milestone outside the inn that records the 21 miles to Manchester and 17 miles to Sheffield. The low stone-built inn is an ideal place to stop for refreshment. Food is served most days of the week and is a range of accommodation is available.

FAIRBROOK, NEAR KINDER SCOUT

TOURIST INFORMATION CENTRES

Holmfirth
49–51 Huddersfield Road.
Tel: 01484 222444

Saddleworth
High Street, Uppermill, Oldham.
Tel: 01457 870336

NATIONAL PARK CENTRES

Visit all under www.peakdistrict.gov.uk

Castleton
Cross Street (main car park).
Tel: 01433 620679

Edale
Fieldhead (right of road from Edale Station to village).
Tel: 01433 670207

Fairholmes (Derwent Valley)
Tel: 01433 650953

PLACES OF INTEREST

Blue John Cavern
1m (1.6km) west of Castleton via Winnats Pass.
Tel: 01433 620638;
www.bluejohn-cavern.co.uk

Last of the Summer Wine Exhibition
Huddersfield Road, Holmfirth. Tel: 01484 681408

Peak Cavern
Castleton, village centre.
Tel: 01433 620285;
www.devilsarse.com

Peveril Castle
Castleton. Tel: 01433 620613;
www.english-heritage.org.uk

Saddleworth Llama Trekking & Animal Farm
High Oxhey Farm, Denshaw.
Tel: 01457 810186; www.saddleworthllamatrekking.com
Walk with llamas in the moors and valleys of Saddleworth.

Saddleworth Museum
High Street, Uppermill.
Tel: 01457 874093; www.saddleworthmuseum.co.uk

Speedwell Cavern
0.5 miles (800m) west of Castleton at Winnats Pass.
Tel: 01433 620512;
www.speedwellcavern.co.uk

Treak Cliff Cavern
0.75 miles (1.2km) west of Castleton. Tel: 01433 620571;
www.bluejohnstone.com

SHOPPING

Castleton
Farmers market, first Sun each month.

Glossop
Indoor market, Thu; indoor and outdoor market, Fri and Sat.

Holmfirth
Craft market, Sat and Bank Hols.
Farmers Market, 3rd Sun each month.
General market, Thu.

LOCAL SPECIALITIES

Blue John Jewellery
Speedwell Caverns Ltd, Winnats Pass, Castleton.
Tel: 01433 620512
Also available from other local outlets.

Craft workshops
Glossop Craft Centre, No 1 Smithy Fold, off High Street East, Glossop.
Tel: 01457 863559;
www.glossopmaycrafts.co.uk

SPORTS & ACTIVITIES

ANGLING

Arnfield Reservoir
Tintwistle.
Tel: 01457 856269; www.arnfield-fly-fishery.com

BOAT TRIPS

Saddleworth
Pennine Moonraker Canal Cruises
Tel: 0161 652 6331; www.saddleworth-canal-cruises.co.uk

CAVING

Edale
YHA Activity Centre, Rowland Cote, Nether Booth.
Tel: 01433 670302;
www.yha.org.uk

Hathersage
Rock Lea Activity Centre, Station Road.
Tel: 01433 650345;
www.iain.co.uk

COUNTRY PARK

Etherow Country Park, George Street, Compstall, Stockport.
Tel: 0161 4276937

CYCLING

Longdendale Trail

This is a 6-mile (9.7km) multi-user trail between Hadfield and the Woodhead Tunnels.

The Sett Valley Trail

This trail runs for 2.5 miles (4km) from New Mills to Hayfield.

CYCLE HIRE

Glossop

Peak Tours
Tel: 01457 851462;
www.peak-tours.com

Hayfield

Old Railway Station.
Tel: 01663 746222;
www.peakdistrict.org

GUIDED WALKS

National Park Walks with a Ranger

For more details contact the Peak District National Park. Tel: 01629 816200;
www.peakdistrict.org.uk

New Mills

Peak Outdoor Training, Marsh Road, New Mills, Derbyshire. Tel: 01663 743278 www.peakoutdoortraining.co.uk
Guided walks, also rock climbing, canoeing and other adventure sports:

Peak District

Annual Peak District Walking Festival. Large programme of guided walks held in late Apr/early May. Tel: 0870 444 7275;
www.visitpeakdistrict.com/walk

HANG- AND PARA-GLIDING

Peak Airsports

Joan Lane, Bamford.
Tel: 07703 062721;
www.peakairsports.com

HORSE-RIDING

Edale

Lady Booth Riding Centre.
Tel: 01433 670205

LONG-DISTANCE FOOTPATHS AND TRAILS

The Limestone Way

A 46-mile (74km) route south from Castleton to Rocester (Staffordshire).

The Pennine Bridleway

Aimed at horse-riders and cyclists, but also useful to walkers. A lengthy 350 miles (563km) from Cromford via the Dark Peak to Byrness (Northumberland).

The Pennine Way.

Runs for 256 miles (412km) from Edale to Kirk Yetholm, just over the border in Scotland.

The Sett Valley Trail

This trail runs for 2.5 miles (4km), from New Mills to Hayfield.

ROCK-CLIMBING

Edale

Edale YHA Activity Centre, Rowland Cote, Nether Booth.
Tel: 0870 770 5808

Hathersage

Rock Lea Activity Centre, Peak Activities Ltd, Station Road. Tel: 01433 650345;
www.iain.co.uk

WATERSPORTS

Hathersage

Rock Lea Activity Centre, Peak Activities Ltd, Station Road. Also helicopter rides.
Tel: 01433 650345;
www.iain.co.uk

■ ANNUAL EVENTS & CUSTOMS

For the full programme visit www.visitpeakdistrict.com

Alport Castle

Alport Love Feast in Alport Barn. Access via Heyridge Farm on A57, early Jul.

Castleton

Garland Ceremony, 29 May.

Glossop

Jazz Festival, mid-Jun.
Carnival and Country Fair, early Jul.
Victorian weekend, early Sep.
Well dressing and Padfield Plum Fair, Sep.

Hayfield

Well dressing, mid-Jul.
Sheepdog Trials, Sep.

Holmfirth

Folk Festival, early May.

Hope

Well dressing, late Jun–early Jul.
Sheepdog Trials and Agricultural Show, late Aug.

Saddleworth

Brass band contest, Whit Friday.
Folk Festival, late Jul.
Longwood Thump Rushcart Festival, late Aug.

Tea Rooms

Rose Cottage Café

Cross Street, Castleton, Derbyshire S33 8WH
Tel: 01433 620472; www.rosecottagecastleton.co.uk

Climbing plants decorate the outside of this traditional English teashop. At the rear is a secluded patio. There's an excellent choice of freshly prepared food, including cream teas, grand sandwiches, home-baked cakes, steaming bowls of soup and great coffee.

Jamaica Blue

56 High Street, Uppermill, Saddleworth OL3 6HA
Tel: 01457 870555; www.jamaicablue.co.uk

A stylish café-bar beside the River Tame and close to a museum, canal and parks. The new riverside patio is a peaceful retreat at which to chow down with teas and coffees, sweet treats, ciabattas, snacks or even filling meals.

The Wrinkled Stocking Tea Room

Huddersfield Road, Holmfirth, West Yorkshire HD9 2JS. Tel: 01484 681408; www.wrinkledstocking.co.uk

Cool pastel walls and crisp tablecloths – just what Nora Batty would expect! Located at those famous steps at Compo's house (now an exhibition), indulge in home-baked speciality pastries and cakes and good Yorkshire tea. Sid's Café (Tel: 01484 689610) is a short stroll away, near the church.

Woodbine Café

Castleton Road, Hope, Derbyshire S33 6AA
Tel: 01433 621407; www.woodbine-hope.co.uk

A welcoming, homely stone terraced cottage, with a sheltered tea garden, not far from Hope's distinctive church. Within, it is cosy and tranquil, appetising aromas of home-baking mingling with quiet conversation or the crackle of logs on a winter fire. They also offer B&B.

Pubs

The Church Inn

Pob Green, Uppermill (Saddleworth) OL3 6LW
Tel: 01457 820902

Splendid food is twinned with tasty beers brewed in the cellar. Memorabilia from the Rushcart Festival held each August is scattered about. Views from this most welcoming gritstone pub, high above the Tame Valley are stunning. As you might guess from its name, it is situated next to the church.

Cheshire Cheese Inn

Edale Road, Hope, Derbyshire S33 6ZF
Tel: 01433 620381

A compact, cheerful local with a warm welcome guaranteed. The landlord is keen on stocking beers from some of the Peak District's many microbreweries and offers an ever-changing menu using local produce whenever possible.

Pack Horse Inn

Mellor Road, New Mills, Derbyshire SK22 4QQ
Tel: 01663742365; www.packhorseinn.co.uk

High above New Mills, the inn has an enviable position with views to the great moorland plateau of Kinder. It's a lovely stone-built place with a growing reputation for good wholesome food and an eclectic choice of real ales.

The Royal Hotel

Market Street, Hayfield, Derbyshire SK22 2EP
Tel: 01663 741721; www.theroyalhayfield.co.uk

At the hub of the village, this grandiose inn has a patio where you can enjoy the local beers and take in the views of Kinder Scout. Inside, find a peaceful corner and tuck in to filling pub grub – there's usually a good fish menu.

PEAK DISTRICT NATIONAL PARK INFORMATION POINT

Peak District National Park Headquarters
Head Office, Aldern House, Baslow Road, Bakewell.
Tel: 01629 816200; www.peakdistrict.gov.uk

OTHER INFORMATION

Angling
Numerous opportunities for fishing on farms, lakes and rivers. Permits and licences are available from local tackle shops and TICs.

Cheshire Wildlife Trust
Bickley Hall Farm, Bickley Malpas, Cheshire SY14 8EF
Tel: 01948 820728; www.cheshirewildlifetrust.co.uk

Derbyshire Wildlife Trust
East Mill, Bridge Foot, Belper DE56 1HX. Tel: 01773 881188; www.derbyshirewildlifetrust.org.uk

English Heritage
Canada House, 3 Chepstow Street, Manchester.
Tel: 0161 242 1400; www.english-heritage.org.uk

Environment Agency
PO Box 544, Rotherham South Yorkshire S60 1BY
Tel: 08708 506506

The National Trust
East Midlands Regional Office, Clumber Park Stableyard, Worksop, Nottinghamshire S80 3AZ
Tel: 01909 4863411; www.nationaltrust.org.uk

Natural England
"Endcliffe", Deepdale Business Park, Ashford Road, Bakewell DE45 1GT.
Tel: 0300 060 2228

Parking
Most urban and many rural car parks in Derbyshire and the Peak District area are pay-and-display. Period visitors' parking tickets are available to personal callers from National Park Visitor Centres and cycle hire centres, or apply in writing to the Peak District National Park Head Office at Bakewell, Derbyshire.

Places of Interest
There will be an admission charge unless otherwise stated. We give details of just some of the facilities within the area covered by this guide. Further information can be obtained from local TICs or the web.

Public Transport
'Derbyshire Wayfarer' allows one day's unlimited travel on all local buses and trains. Details from Derbyshire County Council, Public Transport Dept.
Tel: 01629 536738
Bus services in Derbyshire Tel: 0871 200 2233; www.derbysbus.info
GMPTE Tel: 0161 244 1000; SYPTE Tel: 01709 515151
Rail information. Tel: 08457 484950

Staffordshire Wildlife Trust
The Wolseley Centre, Wolseley Bridge, Stafford ST17 0WT.
Tel: 01889 880100; www.staffordshirewildlife.org.uk

Weather
Tel: 0906 850 0412; www.weathercall.co.uk

ORDNANCE SURVEY MAPS

SOUTHERN DALES
Landranger 1:50,000; Sheets 119, 128
Explorer 1:25,000; Sheet OL24

BUXTON & WESTERN MOORS
Landranger 1:50,000; Sheets 118, 119
Explorer 1:25,000; Sheets OL1, OL24

WHITE PEAK
Landranger 1:50,000; Sheet 119
Explorer 1:25,000; Sheets OL1, OL24

DERWENT VALLEY & EASTERN MOORS
Landranger 1:50,000; Sheets 110, 119
Explorer 1:25,000; Sheets OL1, OL24

DARK PEAK
Landranger 1:50,000; Sheet 110
Explorer 1:25,000; Sheet OL1

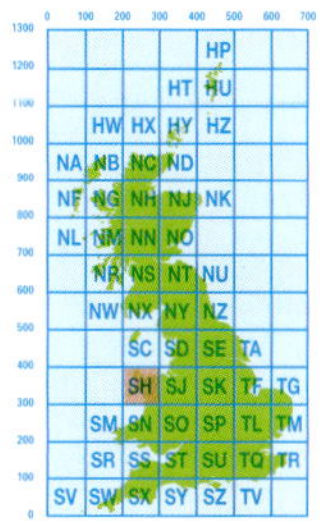

The National Grid system covers Great Britain with an imaginary network of grid squares. Each is 100km square in area and is given a unique alphabetic reference, as shown in the diagram above.

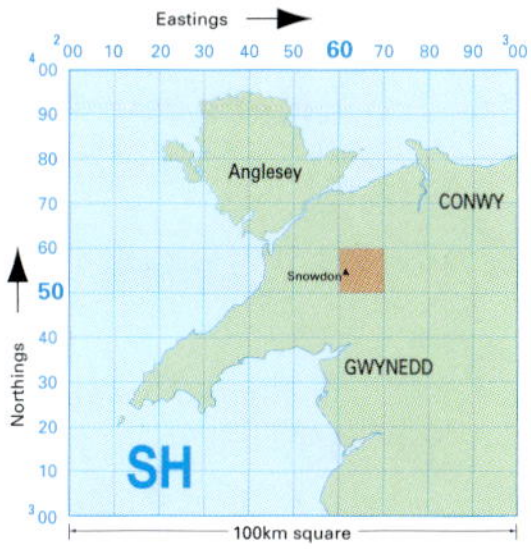

These squares are sub-divided into one hundred 10km squares, identified by vertical lines (eastings) and horizontal lines (northings). The reference for the square a feature is located within is made by adding the numbers of the two lines which cross in the bottom left corner of that square to the alphabetic reference (ignoring the small figures). The easting is quoted first. For example, SH6050.

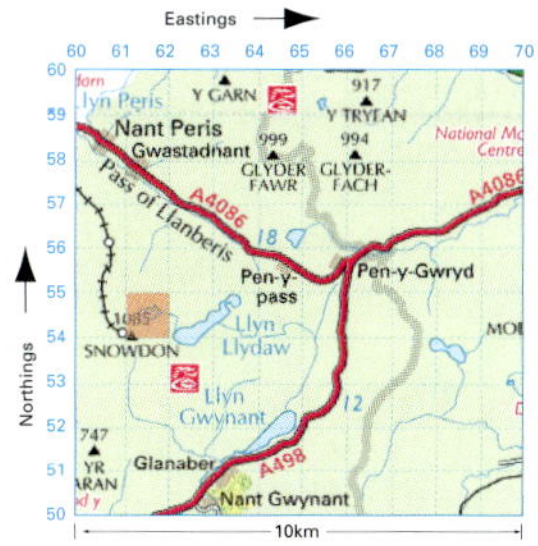

For a 2-figure reference, the zeros are omitted, giving just SH65. In this book, we use 4-figure references, which allow us to pinpoint the feature more accurately by dividing the 10km square into one hundred 1km squares. These squares are not actually printed on the road atlas but are estimated by eye. The same process is carried out as before, giving an enhanced reference of SH6154.

Key to Atlas

- Motorway with number
- Motorway service area
- Motorway toll
- Motorway junction with and without number
- Restricted motorway junctions
- Motorway and junction under construction
- Primary route single/dual carriageway
- Primary route destinations
- Roundabout
- Distance in miles between symbols
- Other A Road single/dual carriageway
- B road single/dual carriageway
- Unclassified road single/dual carriageway
- Road tunnel
- Toll
- Road underconstruction
- Narrow Primary route with passing places
- Steep gradient
- Railway station and level crossing
- Tourist railway
- National trail
- Forest drive
- Heritage coast
- Ferry route
- Walk start point
- Cycle start point
- Tour start point
- Abbey, cathedral or priory
- Aquarium
- Castle
- Cave
- Country park
- County cricket ground
- Farm or animal centre
- Garden
- Golf course
- Historic house
- Horse racing
- Motor racing
- Museum
- Airport
- Heliport
- Windmill
- National Trust property
- National Trust for Scotland property
- Nature reserve
- Other place of interest
- Park and Ride location
- Picnic site
- Steam centre
- Ski slope natural
- Ski slope artifical
- Tourist Information Centre
- Viewpoint
- Visitor or heritage centre
- Zoological or wildlife collection
- Forest Park
- National Park (England & Wales)
- National Scenic Area (Scotland)

SD
Rawtenstall
Bacup
Clough Foot
Edgeside
Rockliffe
Britannia
Lumbutts
Knowle Wood
Walsden
Sowerby Bridge
Norland Town
Copley
Greetland
Longley
Lumb
Mill Bank
Soyland Town
Holywell Green
Barkisland
Stainland
Ripponden
Rishworth
Krumlin
Sowood
Outlane
Scapegoat Hill
East Lancashire Railway
Stacksteads
Cowpe
Boarsgreave
Shawforth
Bottoms
Warland
Chatterton
Edenfield
Facit
Millgate
Whitworth
Turn
Shuttleworth
Calderbrook
Summit
Wardle
Shore
Calderbrook
Catley Lane Head
Broadley
Littleborough
Lydgate
Durn
Rishworth Moor
Deanhead
Pole Moor
Scammonden
Bolster Moor
Bradshaw
Slaithwaite
Linthwaite
Nuttall
Red Lumb
Wolstenholme
Healey
Syke
Smallbridge
Dearnley
Saddleworth Moor
Hollingworth Lake
Smithy Bridge
Rakewood
Summerseat
Norden
Shawclough
Cutgate
Greenmount
Walmersley
ROCHDALE
Firgrove
Milnrow
Moss Moor
Standedge Experience
Hill Top
Marsden
Helme
Limefield
Bamford
Higher Ogden
Motorman's Café
Chesham
BURY
Hooley Bridge
Crimble
Sudden
Lower Place
Balderstone
Haugh
Newhey
Close Moor
Elton
Heywood
Castleton
Burnedge
Crompton Fold
Shaw
Denshaw
Meltham
Slackcote
Redvales
Hopwood
Slattocks
Summit
Tandle Hill
Royton
Clough Grains Bar
Delph
Harrop Dale
Diggle
Hollins
Birch
Top of Hebers
A627(M)
Chadderton Fold
Long Sight
Heyside
Moorside
Thurston Clough
New Delph
Dobcross
Radcliffe
Chapel Field
Whitefield
Simister
Langley
Chadderton
Besses o' th' Barn
Stand
Southead
Austerlands
Uppermill
Holme
MIDDLETON
Heaton Hall
Lees
Grotton
Grasscroft
Greenfield
Saddleworth Moor
582 BLACK HILL
Clifton
Prestwich
Blackley
OLDHAM
Alt
Pitses
Park Bridge
Pendlebury
Rainsough
Sedgley Park
Crumpsall
Moston
Failsworth
Mossley
Swinton
Cheetham Hill
Harpurhey
Bardsley
Broughton
Charlestown
Newton Heath
Woodhouses
Daisy Nook
Luzley
Hazelhurst
Heyrod
Carrbrook
537 FEATHERBED MOSS
Pennine Way
Strangeways
Miles Platting
Ashton-under-Lyne
Millbrook
Crowden
MANCHESTER
Droylsden
Weaste
Eccles
SALFORD
Guide Bridge
Stalybridge
Copley
Roe Cross
Dukinfield
Hollingworth
Tintwistle
Hadfield
Padfield
Ardwick
Audenshaw
Hulme
Gorton
Mottram in Longdendale
TRAFFORD PARK
Old Trafford
Rusholme
Woolley Bridge
Gamesley
Old Glossop
Godley
Stretford
Denton
Hyde
Hattersley
Glossop
Chorlton-cum-Hardy
Fallowfield
Levenshulme
Reddish
Haughton Green
Gee Cross
Broadbottom
Simmondley
Snake Pass 512
Woodley
Werneth Low
Charlesworth
Charlestown
Withington
Burnage
Heaton Chapel
South Reddish
Didsbury
Sale
Heaton Norris
Bredbury
Romiley
Holehouse
Chisworth
544 FEATHERBED TOP
Heaton Mersey
Lower Bredbury
Etherow
Compstall
Chunal
Abbot's Chair
Wythenshawe Hall
Northenden
STOCKPORT
Mill Brow
Timperley
Cheadle Heath
Marple Bridge
Rowarth
Brookhouses
Offerton
Heaviley
Davenport
Stepping Hill
Marple
Cheadle
Mellor
Little Hayfield
Altrincham
Gatley
Adswood
Cheadle Hulme
Hazel Grove
Hawk Green
Aspenshaw
Thornsett
636 KINDER SCOUT
Hale
Davenport Green
Wythenshawe
Heald Green
Windlehurst
Strines
Birch Vale
New Mills
Hayfield
Smithy Green
Disley
Low Leighton
569 BROWN KNOLL
Heyhead
Bramhall
Poynton
High Lane
Manchester
Styal
Hollinlane
Higher Disley
Newtown
Thorns Green
Quarry Bank Mill
Handforth
Hockley
Furness Vale
Chinley
Malcoff
Midway
Lyme Park
Wash
Chestnut Centre
Morley
Wardsend
Whaley Bridge
Morley Green
Woodford
Skellorn Green
Booth Green
Horwich End
Tunstead Milton
Chapel Milton
Wilmslow
Davenport Green
Adlington
Dean Row
Lower Crossings
Chapel-en-le-Frith
Macclesfield Canal
411 SPONDS HILL
Taxal
Lindow End
Mottram St Andrew
Whiteley Green
Kettleshulme
Cockyard
Knolls Green
Rows of Trees
Pott Shrigley
Dunge Valley
Fernilee
Dove Holes
Great Warford
Alderley Edge
Hough
Hare Hill
Bollington
Bollington Cross
Combs
501
R. Bollin
M60
M62
M66
M56
M67
A58
A6
A523
A6033
A628
A6015
A635
A624
A538
A34
A555
A5102
A5149
A560
A6017
A57
A62
A664
A671
A672
A640
A663
A669
A670
A680
A681
A56
A576
A6104
A635
A627
A6018
B6105
B6106
B6107
B6113
B6114
B6138
B6194
B6197
B6222
B6393
B6167
B6178
B6175
B6101
B6104
B6062
B5470
B5358
B5166
B5085
B5169
B5145
B5093
B6170
3
4

Brighouse
Clifton
Hartshead
Liversedge
Norristhorpe
Roberttown
Crossley
Batley
Dewsbury
Chidswell
Kirkhamgate
Wrenthorpe
Outwood
Newton Hill
Stanley
Altofts
Normanton
Hopetown
Elland
Rastrick
Lower Edge
Bradley
Mirfield
Northorpe
Ravensthorpe
Savile Town
Earlsheaton
Gawthorpe
Flushdyke
Ossett
Healey
South Ossett
Horbury
Thornhill Lees
Thornhill
Whitley Lower
Middlestown
Netheroyd Hill
Sheepridge
Colne Bridge
Upper Heaton
Upper Hopton
Birchencliffe
Fartown
Lindley
HUDDERSFIELD
Edgerton
Kirkheaton
Hill Side
Cowmes
Houses Hill
Grange Moor
Overton
Flockton Green
Netherton
Great Cliffe
Crigglestone
Durkar
Walton
Calder Grove
Lupset
Wakefield
Kirkthorpe
Heath
Warmfield
New Sharlston
Sharlston Common
Sharlston
Nostell Priory
Crofton
New Crofton
Foulby
Sandal Magna
Milnthorpe
Belle Vue
Redbeck Motel
Featherstone
Moldgreen
Almondbury
Lower Houses
Berry Brow
Newsome
Fenay Bridge
Lepton
Rowley Hill
High Green
Flockton
Emley Moor
Emley
Midgley
West Bretton
National Coal Mining Museum
Yorkshire Sculpture Park
Woolley
Woolley Edge
Notton
Royston
Havercroft
South Hiendley
Cold Hiendley
Felkirk
Shafton
Shafton Two Gates
Brierley
Carlton
Staincross
Applehaigh
Crosland Hill
Netherton
Armitage Bridge
Dogley Lane
Highburton
Roydhouse
Kirkburton
Shelley
Skelmanthorpe
Kirklees Light Railway
Clayton West
High Hoyland
Darton
Crosland Edge
Meltham Mills
Honley
Farnley Tyas
Brockholes
Thurstonland
Shelley Far Bank
Lower Cumberworth
Scissett
Kexbrough
Mapplewell
Blacker
New Lodge
Sid Cop
Upper Cudworth
Cudworth
Grimethorpe
Netherthong
Fulstone
Shepley
New Mill
Wooldale
Upper Cumberworth
Denby Dale
Cannon Hall Open Farm
Cawthorne
Barugh
Smithies
Monk Bretton
BARNSLEY
Monk Bretton Priory
Holmfirth
Scholes
Jackson Bridge
Hepworth
Birds Edge
High Flats
Lower Denby
Upper Denby
Tivy Dale
Barugh Green
Gawber
Higham
Hoyle Mill
Stairfoot
Little Houghton
Middlecliff
Longley
Silkstone
Noblethorpe
Hoylandswaine
Dodworth
Ardsley
Darfield
Millhouses
Victoria
Ingbirchworth
Hade Edge
Crow Edge
Thurlstone
Silkstone Common
Dodworth Green
Dodworth Bottom
Worsbrough Dale
Low Valley
Broom Hill
Winscar Reservoir
Carlecotes
Millhouse Green
Spring Vale
Four Lane End
Stainborough
Worsbrough Bridge
Wombwell
Worsbrough
Townhead
Penistone
Hood Green
Wentworth Castle
Crane Moor
Blacker Hill
Hemingfield
Dunford Bridge
Oxspring
Thurgoland
Birdwell
Hoyland Common
Jump
Brampton
Cubley
Langsett
Snowden Hill
Dean Head
Hermit Hill
Pilley
Hoyland Nether
Wath
Woodhead
Upper Midhope
Midhopestones
Green Moor
Finkle Street
Wortley
Tankersley
Upper Tankersley
Elsecar
Elsecar Workshops
Harley
Wentworth
PEAK DISTRICT
Howden Moors
Garden Village
Deepcar
Stocksbridge
Howbrook
Bromley
High Green
Chapeltown
Hood Hill
Barley Hole
Nether Haugh
628 BLEAKLOW HILL
Bolsterstone
Wigtwizzle
Ewden Village
546 MARGERY HILL
Thorpe Hesley
Scholes
Wharncliffe Side
Burn Cross
Whitley
Thorpe Common
Brightholmlee
Howden Reservoir
Grenoside
Ecclesfield
Dropping Well
Kimberworth
Blackburn
Hill Top
R Alport
Bradfield
Oughtibridge
Birley Carr
Shiregreen
Wincobank
Meadowhall
Tinsley
NATIONAL PARK
Worrall
Parson Cross
Snake Pass Inn
ROAD CLOSED SAT/SUN/ BH MON
Derwent Reservoir
Low Bradfield
Ughill
Stacey Bank
Grimesthorpe
Carbrook
Brinsworth
Greenland
PEAK
Dungworth
Woodland View
Owlerton
Walkley
Attercliffe
Don Valley
Catcliffe
Load Brook
Ladybower Reservoir
Stannington
Crookes
Handsworth
Pennine Way
Edale
476 LOSE HILL
464 WIN HILL
457 HIGH NEB
Redmires Reservoir
Fulwood
SHEFFIELD
Arbourthorne
Richmond
Woodhouse
Barber Booth
Blue John Cavern
Mam Tor
Treak Cliff Cavern
Hope
Aston
Thornhill
Bamford
Ringinglow
Brincliffe
Ecclesall
Millhouses
Intake
Hollins End
Hackenthorpe
Whirlow
Castleton
Peveril Castle
Speedwell Cavern
Peak Cavern
Smalldale
Brough
Shatton
Hathersage
Hathersage Booths
Norton
Gleadless
Highlane
Brick Houses
Abbeydale
Dore
Beauchief
Ridgeway
Jordanthorpe
Mosborough
Bradwell
Abney
Old Dam
Leadmill
Totley Brook
Coal Aston
Troway
Ford
Coplow Dale
Leam
Upper Padley
Eyam Moor
Longshaw Estate
Totley
Mickley
Dronfield Woodhouse
Stubley
Summerley
Marsh Lane
Apperknowle
Little Hucklow
Great Hucklow
Windmill
Bretton
Grindlow
Nether Padley
Dronfield
West Handley
Middle Handley
Holmesfield
Unstone
0 5 miles
0 10 km
SE
M1
A616
A628
A629
A61
A57
A635
A636
A637
A638
A642
A644
A62
A6102
A6135
A6187
A6013
A625
B6001
B6049
B6054
B6521

Poynton
Hockley
Higher Disley
Furness Vale
Newtown
Whaley Bridge
Chinley
Malcoff
Mam Tor
Treak Cliff Cavern
Castleton
Peveril
Smalldale
Speedwell Cavern
Peak Cavern
Hollinlane
Handforth
Midway
Wardsend
Macclesfield Canal
Lyme Park
Horwich End
Tunstead Milton
Chapel Milton
Wash
Chestnut Centre
Sparrowpit
Old Dam
Dean Row
Adlington
Booth Green
Bollington Cross
Bollington
Pott Shrigley
Whiteley Green
Mottram St Andrew
Hough
Hare Hill
Prestbury
Watermill
Kerridge
Kerridge-end
Rainow
Tytherington
Higher Hurdsfield
Gincloug
Hurdsfield
Longmoss
Henbury
Broken Cross
Macclesfield
Tegg's Nose
Gurnett
Langley
Sutton Lane Ends
Forest Chapel
Siddington
Warren
Gawsworth
Highlane
Oakgrove
Marton
Rode Heath
North Rode
Eaton
Bosley
Wildboarclough
SHUTLINGSLOE
Allgreave
Wincle
Danebridge
SPONDS HILL
411
Kettleshulme
Dunge Valley
Taxal
Fernilee
Goyt Valley
Combs
Chapel-en-le-Frith
Lower Crossings
Dove Holes
Peak Forest
Little Hucklow
Windmill
Copley Dale
HOB TOR
501
SHINING TOR
559
Cat and Fiddle
515
Burbage
Poole's Cavern
Buxton
Fairfield
Upper End
Tunstead
Smalldale
Peak Dale
Wheston
Tideswell
Hargatewall
Wormhill
Miller's Dale
King Sterndale
Blackwell
Priestcliffe
Priestcliffe Ditch
Cowdale
Staden
Solomon's Temple
Harpur Hill
AXE EDGE
551
Taddington
Chelmorton
Flagg
Sheldon
Pomeroy
Monyash
Earl Sterndale
Gamballs Green
R Dove
Flash
Hollinsclough
Longnor
Crowdecote
Fawfieldhead
Pilsbury
Arbor Low Stone Circle
PEAK DISTRICT NATIONAL PARK
Havannah
Congleton
Key Green
Buglawton
Woodhouse Green
THE CLOUD
Timbersbrook
Rushton Spencer
Heaton
Hightown
Whitemoor
Mossley
Newtown
373
GUN HILL
505
THE ROACHES
Upper Hulme
Meerbrook
Tittesworth Reservoir
Brund
Sheen
Wiggenstall
Heathcote
Hartington
Hulme End
Biggin
Newhaven
River Dove
Poolfold
Biddulph Grange Garden
Rudyard Reservoir
Little Moreton Hall
Biddulph
Biddulph Moor
Gillow Heath
Mow Cop
Mow Cop (folly)
Robin Hill
Rudyard
Abbey Green
Thorncliff
Upper Elkstone
Lower Elkstone
Warslow
Ecton
R Hamps
Brindley Mill
Leek
Ball Haye Green
Horton
Lask Edge
Rock End
Greenway
Mount Pleasant
Harriseahead
Brown Lees
Newchapel
Blackwood Hill
Dunwood
Ladderedge
Bradnop
Onecote
Butterton
Alstonefield
Wetton
Grindon
Hope
Milldale
Stanshope
Dove Dale
R Manifold
Kidsgrove
Packmoor
Goldenhill
Brown Edge
Endon Bank
Longsdon
Lowe Hill
Morridge Side
Ford
Great Chell
Ball Green
Norton in the Moors
Stockton Brook
Endon
Horsebridge
Stanley
Flint Mill
Deep Hayes
Cheddleton Heath
Basford Green
Cheddleton
Back o' th' Brook
Waterfall
Ilam
Tunstall
Bradeley
Baddeley Green
Smallthorne
Stanley Moor
Tompkin
Bagnall
Baddeley Edge
Above Church
Winkhill
Burslem
Cobridge
Porthill
Wolstanton
Milton
Northwood
Central Forest Park
Armshead
Wetley Rocks
Churnet Valley Railway
Consall
Ipstones
Waterhouses
Cauldon
Calton
Ilam Park
Blore
Thorpe
Hanley
Etruria
May Bank
Bucknall
Werrington
Cellarhead
Hazles
Foxt
Cauldon Lowe
Caldon Canal
Froghall
Hollins
Upper Cotton
Swinscoe
Mapleton
Ashbourne
Hartshill
Hulme
Blakeley Lane
Kingsley
Whiston
Near Cotton
Stanton
Ramshorn
Mayfield
Middle Mayfield
Stoke-upon-Trent
STOKE-ON-TRENT
Fenton
Whiston Eaves
Oakamoor
Farley
Wootton
Upper Ellastone
Church Mayfield
Trent Vale
Weston Coyney
Cookshill
Dilhorne
Cheadle
Threapwood Head
Alton Towers
Ellastone
Lower Ellastone
Snelston
Longton
Dresden
Caverswall
Meir
Foxfield Light Railway
Threapwood
Alton
Quixhall
Norbury
Hanford
Blurton
Lightwood
Forsbrook
Freehay
Mobberley
Bradley in the Moors
Denstone
Roston
Trentham
The Wedgwood Story
Blythe Bridge
Blythe Marsh
Draycott in the Moors
Upper Tean
Greatgate
Croxden
Abbey
Rocester
Meir Heath
Rough Close
Stallington
Cresswell
Hollington
Saverley Green
Lower Tean
Checkley
Marston Montgomery
Barlaston
Fulford
Cornbridge
Foston Brk
A555
A5149
A5102
B5358
B5166
A538
B5087
B5470
B6062
A6
A5004
A623
B6049
A5270
A537
A536
B5392
A523
A54
A34
A527
A53
B5053
A515
B5054
A520
A522
A521
A52
B5051
B5417
B5032
B5030
A50
A5007
A5272
A500
B5490
A5035
B5029
A519
P+R
90
00
10
80
70
60
50
40
SJ
1
2
3
4
5

Thornhill
Bamford
Ringinglow
Ecclesall
Millhouses
P+R
A61
Hollins End
Intake
Hackenthorpe
A57
Beighton
Holbrook
Rother Valley
B6059
Brough
20
7
Hathersage
Hathersage Booths
30
Abbeydale
Beauchief
Norton
Gleadless
Ridgeway
40
Highlane
Halfway
P+R
Norwood
Woodall
A6187
Dore
Totley Brook
A625
B6068
A6102
Jordanthorpe
Mosborough
Killamarsh
Upperthorpe
Bradwell
Abney
Leadmill
B6001
Upper Padley
Totley
A61
Coal Aston
Troway
Ford
Eckington
80
Woodall
B6049
Eyam Moor
Leam
Longshaw Estate
Mickley
Stubley
B6056
Summerley
Westthorpe
Great Hucklow
Nether Padley
Dronfield
Dronfield Woodhouse
Marsh Lane
Apperknowle
Spinkhill
A6135
Renishaw
Barlborough
Bretton
Grindlow
B6521
A625
B6054
Lidgate
Holmesfield
West Handley
Middle Handley
Emmett Carr
Foolow
Eyam
Grindleford
Froggatt
Horsley-Gate
Cordwell
Cartledge
Unstone
Hundall
Nether Handley
B6053
Millthorpe
Unstone Green
Revolution House
New Whittington
Mastin Moor
30
Stoney Middleton
Calver Sough
Unthank
B6051
Wilday Green
Crowhole
Whittington
Barrow Hill
Woodthorpe
Wardlow
Calver
Curbar
Moorhall
Common Side
Barlow
Staveley
Netherthorpe
Stanfree
Cressbrook
Rowland
B6001
A621
Overgreen
Bole Hill
Sheepbridge
Whittington Moor
Brimington
Shuttlewood
Oxcroft
A623
Hassop
2
Great Longstone
Freebirch
Cutthorpe
Linacres Reservoirs
Newbold
CHESTERFIELD
B6465
Little Longstone
Baslow
B6050
Wigley
A6192
29a
Long Duckmanton
B6418
B6419
Over Woodhouse
Hollins
Old Brampton
New Brampton
Calow
A632
A6020
A619
Pilsley
Chatsworth
Wadshelf
A619
Hasland
Arkwright Town
Castle
Bolsover
6
Dunsa
Edensor
Boythorpe
Cock Alley
M1
Carr Vale
Hills Town
70
Ashford in the Water
Hob Hurst's House
Sutton Scarsdale Hall
Scarcliffe
2
Bakewell
Holymoorside
Walton
Temple Normanton
Palterton
Magpie Mine
B6012
A632
Rylah
Beeley
B6038
B6039
B6425
Heath
Over Haddon
B5055
Little Rowsley
SK
B5057
Wingerworth
A617
Doe Lea
Glapwell
Lathkill Dale
Rowsley
10
Grassmoor
Jcn 29 Truckstop
A6175
29
Stainsby Mill
Haddon Hall
Tinkersley
Northedge
Old Tupton
New Tupton
Holmewood
Alport
Uppertown
North Wingfield
Stainsby
Ault Hucknall
Rowthorne
Youlgreave
Stanton in Peak
R Wye
R Derwent
Brockhurst
A61
Northwood
Alton
Middleton
B5056
Darley Dale
Kelstedge
Waterloo
Astwith
Hardwick Hall
Pleasley
Nine Ladies
Two Dales
Danesmoor
Stanton Lees
Peak Railway
Ashover
Littlemoor
Clay Cross
Hardstoft
Stanley
Birchover
Churchtown
Farley
A632
Fallgate
B6036
Handley
Darley Bridge
Oker Side
Upper Hackney
Milltown
Ogston Reservoir
Pilsley
Dunsill
Dale End
Wensley
Dimple
Stretton
Tibshelf
Fackley
Elton
Winster
Snitterton
Matlock
Ashover Hay
Woolley
Morton
B6014
Stanton Hill
Market House
8
Matlock Bank
Tansley
B6014
Highoredish
Higham
Stonebroom
Newton
Tibshelf
Sutton
60
Brightgate
B5056
Riber
Ashfield
Pikehall
A5012
Heights of Abraham
Starkholmes
A615
Brackenfield
Hallfield Gate
Shirland
Blackwell
Huthwaite
Masson Mills
Matlock Bath
Primrose Hill
B6026
Grangemill
Bonsall
Hilcote
Aldwark
Slaley
Upperwood
Lea
Wessington
Westhouses
B6027
Fulwood
Gulliver's Kingdom
Ible
Amber Row
Toadhole
Cromford Mill
Holloway
B6013
B6406
South Normanton
Longcliffe
Cromford
South Wingfield
Alfreton
B6019
Upper Birchwood
28
National Stone Centre
Derwent Valley Mills
Tramway
Middleton
Bolehill
Crich
B5035
B6019
Pinxton
Brassington
Wingfield Manor
Oakerthorpe
A38
Ballidon
Wirksworth
Little Bolehill
Carr
Lower Birchwood
Whatstandwell
Crich
Park Head
B6600
B6018
Carsington
Hopton
Warmbrook
Swanwick
Somercotes
Selston
Alderwasley
Gorseybank
Pye Bridge
Riddings
B6016
Fritchley
Pentrich
Bullbridge
Bradbourne
Carsington Water
Millers Green
Ambergate
A6
Butterley
Ironville
Jacksdale
Dove Green
B5036
Upper Town
Toadmoor
Lower Hartshay
Midland
Westwood
Bagthorpe
27
Fenny Bentley
B5035
Hognaston
Kirk Ireton
Ashleyhay
Nether Heage
Ripley
Golden Valley
New Brinsley
Underwood
Kniveton
B5023
Belper Lane End
Heage
Upper Hartshay
50
Blackwall
Idridgehay
Greenhillocks
Codnor
Hobsick
A515
Rowfield
Mount Pleasant
Shottle
B6013
Street Lane
Peasehill
Brinsley
Atlow
Biggin
Ireton Wood
Ecclesbourne Valley Railway
Blackbrook
Belper
Whitemoor
Marehay
Cross Hill
Loscoe
Aldercar
A610
A608
B600
Hulland Ward
Hillcliffane
Shottlegate
Openwoodgate
Denby Potteries
Smithy Houses
Moorgreen
Hulland
Turnditch
Cowers Lane
Farnah Green
Bargate
Denby Bottles
Langley Mill
Eastwood
A517
Bradley
Cross o' th' hands
Holbrook Moor
Kilburn
Denby
Heanor
Newthorpe
Hazelwood
Milford
Lower Kilburn
Horsley Woodhouse
Marlpool
New Eastwood
Giltbrook
Ashbourne
Osmaston
Mugginton Lane End
Holbrook
B5023
Horsley
Smalley
Shipley
Awsworth
Makeney
Smalley Green
Shipley
Darley Moor
Mugginton
Duffield
Coxbench
Stanley Common
Cotmanhay
Mapperley
Wyaston
A52
Little Eaton
A38
A6
Smalley Common
A609
Ilkeston
0
5 miles
0
10 km
Shirley
Ednaston
Brailsford Green
West Hallam Common
West Hallam
Morley
A608
Kirk Hallam
Little Hallam
A609
40
Yeaveley
Rodsley
Hollington
Over Burrows
Kedleston Hall
Breadsall
Stanley
Hallam Fields
Alkmonton
Langley Green
Kirk Langley
Allestree
Darley Abbey
20
Thurvaston
Longlane
30
Markeaton
Oakwood
40
Dale
Longford
Lees
Langley Common
P+R
A61
DERBY
6096
Stanton by Dale
Stapleford

Page numbers in bold refer to main entries.

The Automobile Association wishes to thank the following photographers, companies and picture libraries for their assistance in the preparation of this book.

Abbreviations for the picture credits are as follows – (t) top; (b) bottom; (l) left; (r) right; (c) centre; (AA) AA World Travel Library;

1 B Levers/Alamy; 4/5 AA/T Mackie; 8t AA/T Mackie; 8b AA/T Mackie; 9 AA/A Midgley; 10t AA/M Birkitt; 10c AA/M Birkitt; 10b AA/T Mackie; 11t AA/T Mackie; 11b Travel and Places/Alamy; 12 AA/T Mackie; 15tl AA/T Mackie; 15tr AA/T Mackie; 15b AA/T Mackie; 18-19 AA/T Mackie; 21t AA/T Mackie; 21b AA/T Mackie; 22t AA/T Mackie; 22b AA/T Mackie; 23t AA/T Mackie; 23b AA/T Mackie; 31 AA/T Mackie; 34/35 AA/T Mackie; 40 AA/A J Hopkins; 42-43 AA/T Mackie; 45tl AA/T Mackie; 45tr AA/A J Hopkins; 45b AA/A J Hopkins; 46 A Woodacre/Alamy; 47t AA/A J Hopkins; 47c AA/T Mackie; 47b AA/T Mackie; 51 AA/T Mackie; 66 AA/T Mackie; 68-69 AA/T Mackie; 71tl AA/ T Mackie; 71tr AA/T Mackie; 71b AA/T Mackie; 72cl AA/T Mackie; 72cr AA/M Birkitt; 72b AA/T Mackie; 73t AA/P Baker; 73b AA/T Mackie; 82 AA/T Mackie; 90/91 ImagesEurope/Alamy; 93 J Keates/Alamy; 96 AA/T Mackie; 98-99 AA/T Mackie; 101tl AA/T Mackie; 101tr AA/T Mackie; 101b AA/T Mackie; 102c AA/T Mackie; 102b AA/T Mackie; 103t AA/T Mackie; 103b AA/A Midgley; 105 AA/T Mackie; 114 V Lowe/Alamy; 121 AA/A J Hopkins; 126 AA/T Mackie; 128-129 AA/T Mackie; 131tl AA/T Mackie; 131tr AA/T Mackie; 131b AA/M Birkitt; 132 AA/M Birkitt; 133t AA/T Mackie; 133c AA/M Birkitt; 133b AA/T Mackie; 142 AA/T Mackie; 147 C Herring/Alamy; 150 AA/A J Hopkins.

Every effort has been made to trace the copyright holders, and we apologise in advance for an unintentional omissions or errors. We would be please to apply any corrections to any following edition of this publication.